Mid-Century Modern Interiors

Mid-Century Modern Interiors

The Ideas that Shaped
Interior Design in America

LUCINDA KAUKAS HAVENHAND

BLOOMSBURY VISUAL ARTS
LONDON · NEW YORK · OXFORD · NEW DELHI · SYDNEY

BLOOMSBURY VISUAL ARTS
Bloomsbury Publishing Plc
50 Bedford Square, London, WC1B 3DP, UK
1385 Broadway, New York, NY 10018, USA
29 Earlsfort Terrace, Dublin 2, Ireland

BLOOMSBURY, BLOOMSBURY VISUAL ARTS and the
Diana logo are trademarks of Bloomsbury Publishing Plc

First published in Great Britain 2019
Reprinted 2019, 2021

Cover design: Eleanor Rose
Cover image © 2018 Eames Office, LLC

A catalogue record for this book is available from the British Library.

A catalog record for this book is available from the Library of Congress.

ISBN: HB: 978-1-3500-4570-5
           PB: 978-1-3500-4571-2
           ePDF: 978-1-3500-4573-6
           eBook: 978-1-3500-4572-9

Typeset by Integra Software Services Pvt. Ltd.
Printed and bound in Great Britain

To find out more about our authors and books visit www.bloomsbury.com
and sign up for our newsletters.

for Andrew, always

Contents

List of Illustrations

Acknowledgments

Although writing is a particularly singular activity, it is always surprising to see how long a list becomes of people you wish to thank who helped you with a project. In this case the first would be my family—that is my husband, Andrew, who always knew when not to interrupt me, and my faithful rescue dogs, Stanley and Daisy, who lay down at my feet every time I sat down to write as if to protect the process; the "sisters" I've accumulated along the way: Laura Browder, Ann Clarke, Carla Corroto, and Sandy Wheeler, who understood my intellectual life and nourished it; Virginia Commonwealth and Syracuse Universities that supported me during this project and in particular my colleagues there—Dr. Robert Hobbs, my mentor, Christiana Lafazani, who always has been my biggest fan, and Zeke Leonard, who inspires me every day. And finally, my students, whose curiosity and questions are certainly the reason I write.

Preface

They stood like icons in a room that nobody used. Two kidney-shaped love seats, upholstered in a tasteful gray textured wool with tapered blond wood legs peeking out underneath. The tables to match were adjacent—simple lines, straight edges, thin tapered legs, minimal hardware. Across the room was the chair that completed the ensemble, a biomorphic-shaped high-back with the same blond legs, this time in red. I grew up with this furniture and I always wondered about it. Why was it in our house when it didn't really seem to fit? Why was it so different from our neighbor who had a Queen Anne sofa with matching highboy chest? After I was in design school and knew enough to recognize it as modern furniture, I asked my mother why we had it. She stammered and struggled as if caught in an embarrassing moment but finally blurted out, "Well it was expensive at the time!" Her defensiveness only increased my curiosity. She did not admit it, but I knew this furniture had more meaning for her than that. After all, it was her first furniture after she married in 1950 that she brought into her mother's house that she now occupied and that didn't look anything like the furniture she grew up with. No, these pieces matched the furniture I found in a scrapbook hidden in her closet entitled "My Dream House" that had a picture of a modern ranch house neatly glued on its cover. These designs symbolized something to my mother beyond just something to sit on. This furniture had a message and that message was being modern. That my mother was seduced by modern always amazed me. How did that happen in a very small rural community in upstate New York, to a woman who had had no education beyond high school and had never traveled beyond that area? She watched television but never read the newspaper or any books that I can recall. How did the message of modern come to my remote town, reach my mother, and motivate her to possess that furniture at reportedly great expense? As a designer and art historian I have wondered for years about how this could have happened. What was the appeal for my mother who knew nothing of avant-garde art, politics, or philosophy, that led her to choose modern furniture for her new home? What meaning did modern have for my mother and the thousands like her who embraced it in post–Second World War America?

These questions were the impetus for investigating the subject matter of this book. Oddly enough, what my career-long search for answers has revealed to me was not an explanation of my mother's thinking or why she needed that furniture (I might never truly know that), but a new curiosity and interest about the thinking *behind* the designs of those iconic forms that she and others adopted for their homes, offices, and public spaces during the now highly identified period of its heyday—mid-century modern (1940s to 1960s). This shift from investigating the ideas of the users of mid-century modern, like my mother, to exploring the ideas of its designers and creators, happened only after I was fully immersed in the field of interior design as a practitioner and educator and had become acutely aware through that experience of the stereotypes assigned to my discipline as both feminine and decorative. My work in exploring the reasons for the gendering of interior design led me to discover an interesting statement made by Edgar Kaufmann jr. curator of the Good Design shows at Museum of Modern Art in the 1950s. In his booklet written to explain the relatively new profession of interior design to the public "What Is Modern Interior Design?" Kaufmann outlined what he thought were the characteristics that defined the field. The most important identifier, in his opinion, was that interior design was based in "principles, not effects" and that this was what distinguished it from interior decoration. Kaufmann noted that pioneers in the field understood that they "did not want to imitate effects but to follow principles." "This was the decisive change," he stated, "principles, not effects. The road was open to a new idiom of design, destined to express the life of its own times" (Kaufmann jr. 1953: 7).

This differentiation of interior design from interior decorating was an important aspect of my understanding the gendering of my profession and the stereotypes that came with it. It also explained the rationalist approach that interior design aspired to embody, as well as its stress on the importance of the idea of "concept" as essential in its practice. When I was trained in interior design, I was taught, like any other design student today, that concept is the generator of any well-thought-out design and is of primary importance in the design process. Allen Tate and C. Ray Smith's *Interior Design in the Twentieth Century* (1986), which is a technical text on interior design as well as a history book, reiterates this importance of idea as a generator for interior design:

In all sizes and situations of designing interiors—from single room to a complex series of interrelated spaces, … design thinking springs from one notion, one all-encompassing idea. This is called a concept. (Tate and Smith 1986: 97)

Interior designers are taught that design without concept is just form, aesthetics, or decoration. My education hours were spent flushing out concepts as the generator of a design. The discovery of Kaufmann's quote in combination with my personal understanding of the primacy of concept in the design process led me to wonder what the ideas were behind those pieces of modern design that my mother owned and I grew up with. What I also became acutely aware of and interested in was the realization that for the most part there is no way to know what those concepts were. We buy, enjoy, and study design through our interaction with the original, a copy, or pictures of it—these are the major sites of our experience of design—but without knowing what the concept or ideas behind the work were. These concepts are never heavily documented and most often obscured as we get further and further away from the design's inception point. Knowing how important concept is to the making of design made me wonder if not knowing what the ideas that shaped designs were might be a loss. It made me curious about seeing what those ideas were and what might be gained by that. So, I set out to search for them. Since I am an interior designer by training and practice I chose to examine interiors and specifically (because of my mother) what the concepts were driving mid-century modern interiors. I wondered: What went into these designs? What motivated, shaped, and allowed them to be so successful, prominent, and large part of our visual culture, our history, and even of our present tense?

This book documents my attempt to answer those questions. The first part of that process was deciding what to look at. Of the plethora of designs created during this period, which ones should I consider? I knew that an overarching survey would never allow me the time and concentration it would take to understand what was specifically behind every design and that this would require an act of focus. But who or what to focus on? Instead of going to books that were already written on the subject, I explored the design periodicals of the period to see whose names and designs kept rising to the top. The list I culled out of that process of George Nelson, Charles and Ray Eames, Richard Neutra, Florence Knoll, and Russel and Mary Wright includes some of the most prominent designers of modern interiors during this period, noted as such in Kaufmann's 1953 booklet, but also a group that seemed to present a broad range of approaches and influences in the burgeoning field of interior design. In the process of researching this book I tried to look behind the doors of these designer's offices, personal lives, and experiences so I could understand what might have inspired and fed their designs. This took me to libraries; to dig through boxes from archives not knowing exactly what I was looking for; to go back to magazines, articles, diaries, and notes written during the time of certain design's productions; to re-read what other authors and historians had written; and to try to re-look at mid-century modern interiors in a new way by overlaying the motivating ideas that I uncovered as the work progressed. By doing so I discovered that there was not one concept behind the work of these designers, but numerous ones. It became clear to me that mid-century modern is not a generic brand or singular formal aesthetic, but the physical manifestation of the many unique underlying concepts and concerns of its designers, each making their approach and product just little different from the others. There is no one mid-century modern style, but a broad range of attempts to embody interiors and furniture with a new spirit rooted in the designer's intellectual life, curiosity, concerns about past and present, and their visions of what modern living should be.

This book explores those multiple interpretations of mid-century modern by revealing the ideas behind the interiors designed by these five prominent designers/designer partners who contributed to the making of this new field from the 1940s to 1960s. Its aim is to bring to light the motivating ideas, philosophies, and conceptual frameworks that fed those designs and created their unique perspectives. In many ways, this exploration of designers' interests, ideas, and inspirations is ethnographic in that it explores the cultural context behind the designs. It also is an inter-textual approach that puts together the variety of word, ideas, and images—written, spoken, and documented by and about these designers and by and about the people and issues that inspired them. These texts are often laid out side by side here to examine what kind of conclusions can be drawn from their intersection and re-reading. And last, this is a biographic if not almost voyeuristic approach, attempting to peek into and explore the designers' personal life and experience in a very intimate way. All these efforts work to foreground the often-forgotten understanding that design is not created in a vacuum but emerges out of a sea of thinking and explorations in combination with the designer's personal experience that make up what we call the "design process." By bringing these ideas to light and privileging them, this book is different from other histories of mid-century modern that concentrate on the end product—the objects and interiors as used today or recorded through photography or experienced in a museum-like setting, separate from their original intent and ideas. This exploration privileges the back end of the design process, the amorphous material and ideas considered before it became embedded in an object or space and placed in showrooms, homes, offices, magazines, and history books. In attempting to reveal the ideas behind these designs this study hopes to enrich our understanding of those spaces and products, perhaps giving us an even greater attachment to them, in the same way knowing the story behind your grandmother's rocking chair makes it more precious to you. Since this is done at a distance without the advantage of being able to talk to any of the designers considered, this work is speculative of course, drawing on both primary and secondary sources and my own education, experience, and understanding of the designs considered. Knowing the truth of these observations and speculations is impossible. But like the archaeologist digging through the evidences and remains of past civilization my attempt here is to put together my best evidences, to make a kind of sense of them, and to present and share what I have discovered and deduced. Hopefully these conclusions will be both interesting and useful.

Introduction

Mid-century modern is a term that has come to be applied to the significant flourishing of modern design[1] in objects, spaces, and architecture during the Second World War and the postwar rebuilding that happened between the 1940s and 1960s. In this project it refers to work done in the United States, when this country took the lead in both production and consumption of modern design. In America, before the Second World War, the newly emerging field of industrial design, pioneered by Henry Dreyfuss, Norman Bel Geddes, Walter Dorwin Teague, and others, had developed modern products for daily use supposedly generated by rationalist concerns for scientific principles, such as aerodynamics and functionalism. These products designed in the 1930s, ranging from cars to furniture and appliances, often assumed a windswept appearance called "streamlining" that made them seem as if they were responding to the forces of movement. Since the need for streamlining products such as pencil sharpeners and table lamps is dubious at best, it can be easily concluded that the visual qualities of the designs, rather than any improved function and efficiency, took precedence and contributed to their primary purpose of encouraging consumerism to aid economic recovery from the Depression. This concern for stimulating the economy and the United States' self-image through visually modern products continued after the Second World War and was invigorated by the visual links that could be made between modern styling and the technology that helped America win the war. Modern design's clean and simple lines, industrial materials, and mass-producibility could be easily related to the airplanes, rockets, and cars that had brought the country into a period of peace and prosperity. At the same time the techniques and materials created to help the war effort—plastics, molded wood, metal, and fiberglass needed new peacetime uses. The manufacturers of these products took advantage of the moment by promoting new products of modern design. As cultural critic Thomas Hine illustrates in his book about post–Second World War American popular culture, *Populuxe*, the proliferation of "modern" products using "space age," "futuristic," "dynamic," and "militaristic" imagery was the hallmark of the period. Modern styling in contemporary materials for postwar products provided a clearly discernible indicator of America's entry into this new phase of its history, and its promotion became an important strategy for continuing economic growth. Design historian Arthur Pulos posits in his history of design in America, *The America Design Adventure* that the "publicity value" of modern design was essential for its "positive effect on the public morale, and the hope that the development of new products [and their consumption] would boost postwar employment and thus help to offset the predicted depression" (Pulos 1988: 47). This effort was given additional impetus by the many early practitioners of modern design who had emigrated from Europe to the United States in the 1930s and '40s such as Josef Albers, Walter Gropius, Mies van der Rohe, and Eliel Saarinen. But these designers added a new component and a new seriousness to this mix, by bringing with them and integrating into their work their basis in theory and cultural concerns, as well as a strong belief in good design's ability to shape human behavior and the quality of life. From their positions in America's major centers of design education—Yale, Harvard, Illinois Institute of Technology, and Cranbrook—they influenced the ideas of the next generation of designers who shaped the developing practice of modernism and interior design in the United States from the 1930s through the 1960s.

Supported by industry and institutions such as the Museum of Modern Art, the design disciplines worked to develop new products for the modern age in this mid-century period. By as early as the 1930s the emerging practice called "interior design" had become a potent medium for this purpose. In the same way that modern art and architecture rejected the use of historical models as appropriate for their time, interior design rejected the practice of decorating, which was viewed as being based primarily in personal taste and an amateur yet knowledgeable understanding of historical traditions.[2] By embracing the modern movement's concept of "design," as advanced by the Bauhaus in the 1920s and '30s, interior design presented itself in the postwar period as a systematic, intellectual and rational alternative for creating interior spaces for daily use. As Edgar Kaufmann jr. had pointed out in his 1953 explanatory booklet, interior design's foundation, in contrast to interior decorating, was in "principles, not effects" (Kaufmann jr. 1953: 7). Since it was more ephemeral than architecture and more permanent than fashion, interior design provided an interesting middle-ground temporality that made it particularly useful for reflecting the emerging principles that were shaping American society and concerns. At the same time, interior design's materiality and its close relation to daily activity and human behavior facilitated the ability to integrate those principles where they could directly impact daily American life.

Like modern art and architecture, interior design was rooted in concept and modern theoretical ideas that reflected this era's rational search for better understanding of the world and its processes. As Tate and Smith outlined, concept was the important generator for interior design, which was grounded in "facts, experiences, or from the need to solve a problem" (Tate and Smith 1986: 97). To use the word "design" instead of "decoration" in relation to creating interiors, therefore, implies the use of a systematic and rational approach that has its basis in idea not personal preference, just as Kaufmann identified. And so, while historicism and taste were the generators of interior decoration, modern theory and rational ideation were the generators of an emerging field of interior design. By the late 1930s both the discourse and practice of interior design as an alternative to interior decoration had begun to emerge in the United States as the word "design" as well as the phrases "interior design" and "interior architecture" begin to be used instead of "decoration" to refer to interiors in periodicals and magazines. By the 1940s a professional journal devoted totally to the subject of interior design, called *Interiors*, was started. It was followed a decade later by *Interior Design* in 1950. Features about interior designers and interiors in mainstream magazines, such as *Life* and *Better Homes and Gardens*, in the 1950s and '60s furthered the recognition and advancement of the field.

This book explores how the emerging practice of interior design between the late 1930s and the 1960s developed through the efforts of designers from various fields who embraced this systematic and rational approach to creating interiors based on "principles, not effects." In particular, it highlights the work of some of the most prominent designers of modern objects and spaces during this period—Ray and Charles Eames, George Nelson, Richard Neutra, Florence Knoll, and Russel and Mary Wright, who used interior design as a way to explore and express modern issues. This book will not situate these designers within the profession of interior design as it has come to be known and historically documented, however, but rather within the emergent and more fluid discursive field and practice of "designing" interiors that existed during this time and that can be seen as the incubatory period of the profession. From the 1930s through the early 1960s designers from the fields of architecture, art, theater, and industrial design all contributed to the development of interior design practice. Although the modern practice of interior design has often been characterized in histories as a consistent and homogeneous impulse, in reality, particularly during its emergent phase, it embodied many distinct efforts from a variety of divergent directions. In many cases, however, these contributions have not been fully recognized because the practitioner was not labeled as an interior designer and consequently not included as part of this field's established history. The history of this period has also been obscured by the fact that contemporary practices in interior design are often disconnected from theoretical roots. Interior design has developed a more expansive definition in the twenty-first century that includes a range of activities from space planning to home crafts and may focus mostly on the "effects" rather than the underlying "principles" deemed necessary by Kaufmann. As a result, current interior design is a frequently misunderstood concept that often still can be characterized as interior decoration, commercial, fashion based, and reliant on a desire to impress more than transform the world.[3] This work attempts to refocus the study of interior design back on the "principles" that were the generators for interior design during mid-century modern and to reveal the prominent role that a rational and theoretical approach to interior design played during this time period. To do this, this book uses investigative case studies that consider the work of these major designers (or design partners) who used recognizably theoretical approaches to the practice of modern interior design—some historically identified as architects, industrial designers, or furniture designers, but included here because they were leaders in the field at this time.

The first of these are Russel and Mary Wright, who began developing a recognizably modern approach to interiors in the early 1930s. Coming from a background in both theater and industrial design, Russel Wright (1904–76) worked with his wife, Mary Einstein Wright (1904–52) to design appropriate settings for a modern American lifestyle. In their seminal work *Guide to Easier Living* (1950) they promoted a specifically American informality in home designs that were flexible, easily maintained, and intended to nourish physical as well as emotional well-being. The work of Russel and Mary Wright will be studied here as to how interior plans promoted in *Guide to Easier Living* as well as designs for the Wrights' own homes incorporated ideas about national identity and the "new American way of life" being promoted during this period.

The second, Austrian-born Richard Neutra (1892–1970), was a prolific designer of modern buildings in the United States from the 1930s until the 1960s and was working on the West Coast at the same time the Wrights were becoming known on the East Coast. Although generally identified as a disseminator of the International Style, Neutra maintained strong social and behavioral concerns in his work that far surpassed the predominately formalist approach of this style. The work of Neutra will be considered here as to how his particular concern for ideas about behavioral psychology and "therapeutic" design played an important role in the modern domestic interiors he created.

Contemporaries of Neutra, but from the next generation of designers, Ray Kaiser Eames (1912–88) and Charles Eames (1907–78) emerged as leaders in postwar modernism and were known for products designed by the Eames office, such as their molded plywood and fiberglass chairs, acclaimed for their modern technical and aesthetic innovation. The Eameses are included here for their most notable contribution to interior design, the design of their own home in 1949 in Pacific Palisades, California, which has attained iconic status in the history of modernism. The design of the Eames House and other interiors completed by the couple during this period will be examined as to the ways that theoretical ideas about vision, particularly the creation of a new "language of vision" as advanced by Ray Eames's teacher Hans Hofmann and their colleague György Kepes, are expressed in their interior design.

Both the Eameses and their contemporary George Nelson's (1908–86) successes revolved around their designs for the Herman Miller Furniture Company. While the Eameses turned to work more on movies and exhibition design by the 1950s, Nelson continued to work within Herman Miller to further define the modern interior throughout the 1950s and '60s. Although most discussions of George Nelson focus on his career as an industrial designer and design theorist, he is considered here because of the significant work he did designing interiors in the late 1940s and early '50s as documented in Herman Miller's catalogs and advertisements. It will focus on how his interest in the theoretical concerns of Japanese aesthetics and the ideas of prominent thinkers, such as Erich Fromm, José Ortega y Gasset, and Alfred North Whitehead, were incorporated in his effort to create more moral and humane modern living spaces.

An analysis of the work of Florence Schust Knoll (b. 1917) will conclude this book. Knoll was the creator of the Knoll Planning Unit, one of the first interior design firms to specialize in commercial building projects to which Knoll applied her signature style—a stripped-down classicism in a Miesian aesthetic—still considered the epitome of high design. Knoll studied at Cranbrook Academy with Eliel Saarinen and at the Illinois Institute of Technology in Chicago with Mies van der Rohe. In 1943, she became partners with Hans Knoll, whom she later married, and opened the practice of Knoll Associates (later known as Knoll International), which became one of the largest producers and distributors of modern furniture in the postwar period. Knoll's work designing corporate interiors that were developed together with the Knoll Planning Unit in the postwar period will be considered here to discern the theoretical roots of her designs and how they were influenced by her training with Mies van der Rohe and Eliel Saarinen.

It is important to note that each of these designers had offices, with numerous other designers working for them in those offices. In many cases authorship of the interiors considered here cannot necessarily be traced back or confirmed as being solely the idea of the principals of these offices. It is not the purpose of this study to untangle those questions of authorship, however, and in these examinations, I consider the work of the office as representing the principal designers and reflecting their ideas, their design sensibilities, and their voice in any project produced by the office as whole, since records, publications, and other documents of the period rarely name or recognize any supportive staff or collaborative efforts.

The original publications and periodicals of the period, including articles written in *Interiors, Interior Design*, and *Arts and Architecture*, as well as magazines, museum catalogs, and special texts published by the designers, and the materials now located in various archives around the country have constituted the primary source materials for this book. Secondary sources written by experts who have intimately studied these designers such as Stanley Abercrombie's treatise on George Nelson, William Hennessey on the Wrights, Pat Kirkham on the Eames, Bobbye Tigerman on Knoll, and Thomas Hines and Sylvia Lavin on Neutra have been closely examined for clues into what these designers were thinking, embracing, and encountering in their personal and design lives. In addition, this project also has considered the theoretical treatises and writings that were being published and read by the designers during this time, through both primary and secondary sources, such as the work of György Kepes, Eric Fromm, Julius Meier-Graefe, and others. While this book is an historical examination of the texts about this period, written by these designers or about them, it is also a re-reading of those texts in order to ascertain major themes in the design of interiors in general and their specific development in the work of these designers. Biography, social/ cultural history, formal analysis, and intertextual explorations are incorporated here to provide a richer and more complete understanding of the designers, the interiors, and this period of design history. I have purposely overlooked stereotypical characterizations of interior design as they have emerged over the years to dig for a more complete understanding of the discipline and show the important role that "concept" and ideas did play in interior design as an emerging practice. In doing so it hopes not only to begin to understand the principles at work behind the interior designs of mid-century modern but to present a richer, more complete, and more accurate account of this moment in design history and interior design's contribution to it.

1

Russel and Mary Wright: Nostalgic Modern and the "American Way of Life"

There are many Americans who still enjoy or remember eating off a plate from Russel[1] and Mary Wright's *American Modern* china collection. The dinnerware's beautiful sculptural forms, interesting colors, and simplicity graced many a dinner table in the mid-century period. Moderately priced, well designed, fun yet sensible, these Wright designs became one of the hallmarks of the modern, more informal "new American way of life" that the couple helped create and promote. But *American Modern* dinnerware was just a small part of the Wrights' total oeuvre and their life-long efforts to bring modern design to Americans by creating a specifically American approach to design. To that end, the couple built on the work of their predecessors, Frank Lloyd Wright and the American Arts and Crafts movement, and used interior design as a medium to systematically design or direct the careful choice and placement of all items needed for an appropriately American modern home. They documented this strategy in their popular book *Guide to Easier Living* (1950), which gave extensive directions for house planning, buying furniture, and housekeeping procedures. At the root of these efforts and embedded in all their work was the couple's underlying concern, if not fixation, about how design could and should be used to express American character and values.[2] The trajectory of this concern is a long but consistent theme that runs through the Wrights' careers, and from early on ideas about patriotism and American identity were embedded in the Wrights' work, especially in their approach to interior design. These were promulgated in their *Guide to Easier Living* and in the designs of their own highly publicized homes, supporting them toward their goal of providing an alternative to European modernism and an appropriately American kind of modern interior design.

Early explorations

Russel and Mary Wright were not trained as designers but came to the practice from backgrounds in art and theater. Russel Wright, a native Ohioan, was the son of a judge who claimed an illustrious pedigree as a descendant of American Quakers and signers of the Declaration of Independence. Although encouraged to a career in law, his father's profession, Wright began taking art classes at the Cincinnati Academy of Art while still in high school. After he graduated, he continued that study at the Art Students League in New York City for a year before entering Princeton in the fall of 1921. Although he had agreed to begin to study law at Princeton, he soon left it behind to investigate the college's theater program as an outlet for his creativity. He joined the Triangle Club, the theater's support group, and designed sets and directed plays while working on his degree. In the summer of 1923 he lived in Woodstock, New York, and worked at the well-known Maverick Art Colony on its annual theatrical festival designing sets and props. He returned to Princeton in the fall but spent his weekends in New York City working in the theater there. In 1924, he left school to dedicate all his time to that avocation. There, he soon met set designer Aline Bernstein (later mistress to Thomas Wolfe), who became a close friend and mentor and who helped him find various jobs in the theater in the late '20s, including positions at the Neighborhood Playhouse and Laboratory Theatre in New York. In 1927, Wright returned to Woodstock to work again in the Maverick Theater where he met his future wife, Mary Small Einstein, the daughter of a wealthy, socially established family and a distant relative of the famous Albert Einstein. Mary Einstein was a native of New York City, and when she met Wright, she was studying sculpture with the European artist Alexander Archipenko at his summer workshop in Woodstock. Against her family's wishes Einstein married Wright in 1927. The couple lived in Rochester, New York, for a short time while Wright was the stage manager of George Cukor's theater company, but they soon moved back to New York City where they continued to live for most of their lives.

The transition for Russel Wright from theater to industrial design was a common course of action during the late '20s and '30s as the entrepreneurial spirit that rose out of the stock market crash and subsequent Great Depression encouraged the growth of this new design field. The 1933 and 1939 World's Fairs, with their emphasis on technology and the future, added to this impetus. Leaders in the burgeoning field of industrial design such as Norman Bel Geddes, Raymond Loewy, and Joseph Urban, who helped create futuristic visions for these events, all became successful product, furniture, and interior designers by building on their careers and reputations made in theater design. Theater historian Christopher Innes notes:

That this transfer from theater to industrial and architectural design was possible is partly due to the way America prided itself on being the new world, liberated from the hierarchical traditions of European empires. This made it more acceptable for people to cross over from one specialization to another. American industrialists looking for designers to create mansions that would display their status ... liked what they saw on Broadway and sought out stage designers for the job. (Innes 2005: 15)

Russel Wright had apprenticed with Bel Geddes when he was working as a set designer in New York and was well aware of this trend. The Wrights saw the opportunity in this wave of interest and excitement about industrial design and began their work as a team by designing and promoting numerous products for in-home use in the 1930s such as their successful *Informal Accessories* line of aluminum cocktail sets, cups and ice buckets, and other products. While Russel Wright was the primary designer in these efforts, Mary Wright's history and experience with her family's successful textile manufacturing concern gave her a unique understanding of business and of how to market and promote not only their products but themselves as designers. She organized the production, distribution, and sales for all Russel Wright–designed products until her death in 1952. It was her business acumen and energy that pushed her husband's designs in the 1930s to the forefront and provided him with name recognition throughout the United States. Wright biographer William Hennessey says that Mary Wright "must be given credit for a good deal for the work's popular success. Her business sense, as well as her New York social connections and financial resources were of vital importance in getting the design business started" (Hennessey 1983: 23). Although it was Russel Wright's name that went on most of the products and projects, Mary is considered here as a full partner and given credit alongside Russel for all the Wrights' accomplishments in creating modern American design.

American Modern

By the late 1930s, the Wrights became focused on the goal of creating design that expressed specifically American values. The rising popularity of European modernism in the United States and its promotion by manufacturers, department stores, and institutions, such as the Museum of Modern art and others, became something that they began to see as a threat to American design. They became passionately inspired and motivated to "help rid this country of its great Art-inferiority-Complex" (Albrecht, Schonfeld, and Shapiro 2001: 17) and to create a distinctly American identity for design free from

European influences. As their daughter, Ann Wright, related in her preface to the 2001 publication, *Russel Wright: Good Design Is for Everyone*:

> In fact, it was not until I was nine or ten that I even understood there was a "European Style" From my point of view, there was only "Russel Wright Style," which is what we lived and what the rest of the world ought to live, if they didn't already. (Albrecht et al. 2001: 17)

The Wrights' preoccupation with establishing a distinctly American identity was something they shared with many groups of people. Christopher Innes notes that it was a consistent theme and impetus in the theater world as Americans searched for a "real" national identity aligned with the modern world, and that popular catchphrases such as "the American dream" and "the American way of life" became so standard that in 1939 Kaufman and Hart used "The American Way" as the title for one of their Broadway comedies. Set designers turned product and interior designers such as Joseph Urban and Russel Wright grasped the excitement and creative potential of this moment. Innes says that Urban

> was struck by the new conditions he saw around him. He saw that the modern world, emerging so energetically and chaotically in this young and bustling nation, needed its own mode of expression ... traditional styles, which were still being applied haphazardly across America, would not do. Nor would the new European design principles ... None of these reflected the American experience. (Innes 2005: 2)

The Wrights' and Urban's concerns reflected a trend that had been gaining ground in the United States since the early part of the twentieth century. Historian Michael Kammen points out in his extensive work, *Mystic Chords of Memory: The Transformation of Tradition in American Culture* (1991), how a "general and country-wide revival of Americanism" followed the defeat of "Woodrow Wilson's universal idealism" after the end of the First World War. He says that books such as novelist and cultural critic Waldo Frank's *Our America* of 1919 (serialized for the *New Republic* in 1927–1928 as *The Re-Discovery of America: An Introduction to a Philosophy*) as well as historian Stuart Pratt Sherman's essay "The Emotional Discovery of America" (1925) marked the beginning of a trend to "explore and expound upon American tradition." Kammen concludes that "the emotional discovery that took place during the 1920's produced a vulgate of American exceptionalism never before known. The phrase 'strictly American' popped up boastfully throughout the country" (Kammen 1991: 303). With this impetus, in the '20s and '30s the quest not only to create but also to preserve American traditions came to the foreground.

While poet Stephen Vincent Benét, composer Aaron Copland, and artist Thomas Hart Benton were attempting to create their own distinctly American art forms, connoisseurs and collectors such as Henry Ford and Abby Aldrich Rockefeller made the collection and preservation of American traditional arts a new American initiative. While transforming the world with the modern technology of the automobile, Henry Ford became particularly enamored with preserving the American past and its distinct character. Ford began collecting Americana in the early 1920s and soon compiled one of the most comprehensive collections in the United States. In 1922, he purchased the Colonial-era Wayside Inn in Sudbury, Massachusetts, to preserve it for posterity and to educate the American public about their national heritage. From 1927 to 1944 he created a historically based theme park at Greenfield Village in Dearborn, Michigan, that housed his vast collection, which included entire buildings such as Noah Webster's house and the Wright Brothers' bicycle shop. Ford's enthusiasm was highly motivated by an underlying patriotism. When he opened the Henry Ford museum in Dearborn, Michigan, in 1933 he proudly stated: "We have no Egyptian mummies here, nor any relics of the battle of Waterloo nor do we have any curios from Pompeii, for everything we have is strictly American". Similarly, in 1926 John D. Rockefeller began his obsession with restoring Colonial Williamsburg in Virginia, which would eventually house his wife Abby Aldrich Rockefeller's extensive collection of American folk art. Both Rockefeller's and Ford's efforts reflected the commonly held belief that the American past could provide an inspiration for its future. In a letter to Rockefeller, the editor of the *American Collector* framed his appeal to the philanthropist to create a center for American historical research as an imperative national necessity. He stated, "Our heritage from the heroic past must be preserved as continued guidance and inspiration to ourselves and to all mankind" (Kammen 1991: 322).

The economic crisis in the United States precipitated by the market crash of 1929 and the Great Depression seemed only to enhance this need to identify and draw support from American history and character. Paradoxically, at the same time, the need to push the country forward to progressive modern means also came to the forefront, causing a strange collision of both futurist and historical viewpoints. While modern innovations in American industrial design, architecture, and technology were showcased in the futuristic buildings and displays of the 1933 *Century of Progress* International Exhibition in Chicago as well as in the 1939 World's Fair in New York, historical pageants celebrating American history and traditions were also being celebrated in the same venues. As Kammen explains:

The interwar decades were permeated by both modernism and nostalgia in a manner that may be best described as perversely symbiotic. That is each one flourished, in part, as a critical response to the other. Most of the time, however, there was a little if any recognition that an oxymoronic condition persisted: nostalgic modernism. (Kammen 1991: 300)

This so-called nostalgic modernism seemed particularly appropriate during a time when the threat to democracy by Americans' interest in communism in the 1920s and '30s, as well as the outbreak of war in Europe, created a sense of urgency to preserve the nation's past and protect its future. The reality and visibility of this threat allowed notions of patriotism, the importance of tradition, and the preservation of national character come to the forefront as issues and concerns. The need to demarcate clearly American traditions as separate from their European predecessors was also evident. Many like James T. Flexner, a prominent historian and biographer of George Washington, recommended a clean break from European mores in order to find an appropriate national character:

> In these days when European civilization is tearing itself apart much of the torch of culture is being handed to us, but we cannot carry it on adequately merely on the basis of the European tradition which has developed such cancers. We must explore our own past to find other, stronger, roots based on a continental federation, on a peaceful mingling of races, on a hardy and unsophisticated democracy that grew naturally from a hardy and rough environment. (Kammen 1991: 510)

This type of attitude led to a zealous kind of American "exceptionalism"—a unique brand of nostalgic modernism that reconciled modernity with tradition, technology with hand craft, and diversity with a sense of unity—that is evident in American culture in the late 1930s and war years. It occurs in the contemporary reinterpretation of American folk music in compositions of Aaron Copland, the abstracted contemporary American landscape paintings of Charles Sheeler, and the portraits of life in the South in the novels of William Faulkner. The idea that Americans would look to its past traditions for models for its modern future was not considered antithetical but essential. As social critic Lewis Mumford speculated: "Genuine tradition does not stifle but reinforces our interest in the present and makes it easier to assimilate what is fresh and original" (Mumford 1930: 525). Clearly Russel and Mary Wright's own zealous Americanism shares Mumford's sentiment and reflects the country's general preoccupation with both celebrating and clarifying an American identity free from European influences. The pursuit of a particular American character for contemporary design is a consistent theme in all the Wrights' work.

Wright's first clearly nostalgic modern piece was his design for the Cowboy Modern chair of 1932 (Figure 1.1). This strange hybrid was an ergonomically responsive chair constructed of pony skin, painted vinyl, and carved wood. It looked like a crude cross between a Le Corbusier and Duncan Phyfe design, with solid blocky construction that attempted to visually reconcile the rustic craftsmanship of the American frontier with modern styling. Its pony skin,

FIGURE 1.1 *Russel Wright, Cowboy Modern chair, 1932. (Cooper Hewitt, Smithsonian Design Museum/Art Resource, Photo: Mike Radtke @Smithsonian Institution).*

FIGURE 1.2 *Russel Wright, Rendering of* American Modern *Furniture Line,* c. 1935. *(Russel Wright Papers, Syracuse University Libraries).*

wood construction, and moniker also linked it with myths of the American West, the Great Outdoors, and the quintessentially American individualistic lifestyle of the cowboy that was being celebrated by the newly developing Hollywood movie industry in the 1930s. Its inclusion in Wright's early interior spaces, such as his own apartment on East 40th Street in New York in 1937, adds warmth to the design's cool geometric modernity and suggests a sense of history and tradition.

Like the Rockefellers and Henry Ford, the Wrights also turned to themes of the Colonial period for examples of authentic American character. In 1935, Russel Wright designed a line of solid wood furniture for the Conant Ball furniture company that was called *American Modern* (Figure 1.2). In the company's promotional literature, it was described as a "twentieth century interpretation of the spirit behind American Colonial design—a spirit which prompted frank construction and honest simplicity" (Conant Ball Sales Tips, n.d.). The furniture was made of American rock maple and was available in two finishes: a dark one that replicated more traditional furniture and a light one referred to as "blonde," a term coined by Mary Wright that gave a more modern and contemporary feeling to the pieces. More than fifty pieces were available in the traditional or more modern variations. Its flexibility, simplicity, and particularly its integrity of character were all linked to the marketing of the products compatible with American tradition and craftsmanship. The Conant Ball company claimed that the *American Modern* furniture collection

> is the present-day continuation of Colonial American furniture. Built in maple, the wood of our forefathers, it is designed to express in the twentieth century manner, the simplicity and frank construction of American Colonial

furniture. Just as Early American related to Early American times, so does *American Modern* relate to our modern American scene … [we] have … continued and modernized a century old tradition. For *American Modern* is the logical, present-day continuation of Native American Furniture design. (Conant Ball Sales Tips, n.d.)

Wright identified himself as a designer within this continuing American tradition. His publicity consultant, Mary Ryan, in the early 1930s labeled him the "modern Paul Revere," who, like the famous metalsmith in his own time "works for the American market, for American tastes" (Albrecht et al. 2001: 144). In 1935, the Wrights designed nine model rooms for Macy's department store in New York City, which used *American Modern* furniture. Macy's furniture buyer O.L. Overby praised the success of the line: "Our prophecies that these designs of Mr. Wright's were the most important development in American furniture in the last few decades have been fulfilled to the tune of $250,000—Conant Ball's retail sales per year—not to mention the sales of all like designs immediately following suit."

The Wrights posed Russel's furniture designs and their interior ensembles as an American form of modern that was an alternative to both the European and the Scandinavian modern genres that were being imported to the United States during this period. In being particularly American, these products were marketed as more suitable for American lifestyles and tastes. The success of the *American Modern* line of furniture led the Wrights to develop the *American Modern* line of dishware in 1939, which they also promoted as distinctively American. Advertisements stressed its ability to complement "the informality of modern American Life" and called it an "enduring American original" and a new "beloved tradition." These connections were stressed in the products' advertisements by posing images of the dishware side-by-side with specifically American items such as a Thanksgiving turkey, a Mississippi river boat, Edison's phonograph, and a musical score for the *St. Louis Blues* (Figure 1.3).

Conceived as an informal dinnerware that was multi-functional, *American Modern* earthenware re-conceptualized the contemporary place setting by transforming it into innovative organic shapes in distinctive colors that were often capable of being stacked to save space or that could be brought from the refrigerator directly to the dinner table. Wright's designs reduced the total number of dishes one needed, so the line was well-suited to the new smaller-scale and more informal American home. Even more American was the way the line was marketed. "Starter sets" were offered in settings for four, six, and eight that were affordably priced. A thirty-three-piece starter set for six sold for $14.50 in 1939. The Wrights revolutionized the retail dishware industry by also offering each piece on "open stock." A customer could buy each piece

FIGURE 1.3 *Advertisement for* American Modern *at Famous Barr Co., St. Louis from* House and Garden, *1952. (Russel Wright Papers, Syracuse University Libraries).*

individually and mix and match its colors of Coral, Seafoam Blue, Chartreuse, Curry, Granite Gray, White, and Bean Brown to suit their whims. Wright described *American Modern* as being like Coco Chanel's "little black dress" that could be accessorized to assume different personalities on different occasions

(Albrecht et al. 2001: 35). In its flexibility and accessibility it was democratic and catered to American freedom of choice and individualism. Promotional set-ups of *American Modern* dishware in stores often displayed it in-situ in model rooms, thus instructing its user how the dishware could contribute to the total design of the interior space. *American Modern* dinnerware became one of the best-selling tableware lines in history, grossing $150 million in sales during the twenty years it was produced. Its manufacturer, Steubenville Pottery, had to expand its facilities twice to keep up with the demand for it and the china was so popular during the shortages of the Second World War that it caused a frenzy whenever it was available. As Wright once reminisced:

> During the forties, arrivals of shipments at stores such as Gimbel's in New York would cause near riots. Queues as much as two blocks long necessitated calling out the police. On one occasion two women were injured in pressing to get the wares, and were taken to the store dispensary, and after being administered to, they got back into line. (Wright 2001: 28)

American Modern won the American Designers' Institute Award in 1941 for best Ceramic Design of the Year. Popularity of the line diminished in the 1950s however as the market became saturated with it, and production of the chinaware ended when the Steubenville Company closed in 1959, but currently has been revived and is produced by Bauer Pottery in California.

As war loomed in the late 1930s and patriotic sentiments ran even higher, the Wrights found another opportunity for the promotion of their American modern style. In 1940, with the support of First Lady Eleanor Roosevelt, the couple launched their ambitious *American Way* program at Macy's Department Store. The *American Way* was conceived to promote and market modern home furnishing and accessories designed solely by American designers throughout the country. The goals of the program were threefold: first, to mass-produce and make available original designs by American craftspeople; second, to create a national network for the distribution of this material; and third, to create a coordinated, overarching sales campaign for American products and artisans. The Wrights traveled throughout the country searching for products to include in this nationalistic campaign. They found a range of designs that reflected "harmonious design relationships and color combinations" and which, in their opinion, were capable of fostering "unity with freedom to make our own choice—The American Way" (*American Way* Sales Manual 1941: 2). As part of this effort, the Wrights attempted to solve an issue that promoters of American genres had found difficult to reconcile: how to incorporate diverse regionalist influences into an overarching notion of America's presumed national character. The idea that a common tradition provided social cohesion was useful to the country in its time of crisis, but as Kammen points out, religious, ethnic, and regional diversities were often difficult to reconcile. Wright both recognized and attempted to resolve such differences in his promotion of *American Way* products. In the opening paragraphs of this line's sales manual, the Wrights attempted to establish a connection between the products and America's historical past by claiming that they, like their fellow Americans, were descendants of those traditions, which had been appropriately reinterpreted for contemporary life:

> Our Pioneer Americans, given the opportunity, did not hesitate to add to their homes those changes that would make the job easier. With the materials at hand, they made themselves homes that were consistent, charming, and comfortable ... Based upon a continuation and gradual improvement of what we already have in this country, rather than upon either a forced adherence to past periods, or the abrupt introduction or unprecedented ideas, "American-Way" is evolving a valid program of American Design. (*American Way* Sales Manual 1941: 2)

The Wrights then argue that only American designers can truly understand the needs of American life and echo Flexner's call to put aside the emulation of European traditions:

> American designers know us best—through themselves—know our life in the crowded cities, our country-side, our suburbs, tastes, preferences, taboos ... Thus, "American-Way" offers us simple, livable, good looking 20th century American design with little of the cold sophistication of European inspired modern, nor the triteness of "Modernistic" modern. (*American Way* Sales Manual 1941)

The diversity of the products, which are taken from many different regional styles, is emphasized as an important distinctly American characteristic in the Wrights' literature:

> The desire for American crafts is springing up as a result of growing interest and curiosity concerning our own country. At last, we are beginning to appreciate and evaluate our own outstanding native craft skills, in the realization that they are a living commentary on American modes of life— from Indian times, through the period of our Pilgrim fathers and earliest known Spanish settlers, right up to present day existence. (*American Way* Sales Manual 1941)

In recognizing the importance of the chosen products' diversity, the Wrights echo the sentiments of Ruth Suckow, a prominent contemporary novelist known for writing about Midwestern farming life, who posited in "The Folk Idea in American Life":

> No one doubts that there is a common national existence, becoming constantly more of a piece wide-spread throughout the United States .... There is, for instance variety ... But it is all American ... Something deeply homogenous binds together the extravagant differences. (Suckow 1930: 246)

Suckow then claims that American folk traditions play an important role in constructing a true American identity. In a similar way, Russel and Mary Wright conclude that *American Way's* regional diversity makes it particularly American and definitively appropriate for US citizens to use in their homes. In their sales manual, they grouped objects according to region and framed their overview as an "exciting trip through America" that is comparable to "much of the romance and glamour of [a] far-off place." For each region, they included drawings of their selections together with texts highlighting each object's salient contributions to an American character. In each case the items are seen as embodying distinct regional characteristics. They describe the ones from California, for example, as stemming from a "new-world ... [as] glamorous as Hollywood ... not [at all] hidebound by tradition ... "The designs from the Midwest are characterized by as being "simple, frank and unaffected." The New England wares are "grown out of our earliest American homemaking traditions," and manifest "unrivaled precision and workmanship" that lend them "enduring qualities." Objects from New York are sophisticated and avant-garde in material and form. Those from the Northwest are noted for celebrating America's natural resources such as yellow pine, Oregon flax, and American linen. The Southern region's contributions are "unaffected and sincere" and symbolize Southern hospitality and Southern cooking with their "feeling of abundance and plenty," while those from the Southwest reflect the "ruggedness and crude beauty of the terrain" in their "distinct color sense of the region which combines brilliant colors plus natural toned earthy materials" (*American Way* Sales Manual 1941). This highly stereotypical celebration of regional diversity as part of a distinctly American character highlights the products' greatest appeal according to the Wrights, and one that retailers should note when trying to sell the products in order to boost sales. The cover of the sales manual tells its owner to "read carefully if you expect full sales returns from *American-Way*."

Russel and Mary Wright viewed the *American Way's* diversity as a means for the American public to understand and therefore become proud of their nation's character, thus contributing to their almost xenophobic zeal for all things American. Hennessey relates that "in magazines and speeches he

[Russel Wright] condemned American educators for preaching the superiority of European Art. He praised national diversity and exhorted audiences to discover and celebrate America's beautiful landscape, its abundant resources, and its rich heritage" (Hennessey 1983: 47). In the *American Way* program the Wrights advanced a version of nostalgic modernism that celebrates the richness of the country's inventiveness and its historical traditions, as well as its technology and diversity. And all of this, they readily recognized and often stated, was designed by Americans for Americans. As Hennessey describes, "Just as the Bauhaus was a quintessentially European phenomenon, founded on utopian ideas with long English and Continental pedigrees, so the *American Way* in its mixture of romantic, nationalist, populist, and capitalist elements was peculiarly American" (Hennessey 1983: 51). Model rooms with *American Way* products were set up at Macy's store in New York as well as other department stores around the country (Figure 1.4). The Wrights theorized that many Americans felt insecure about their aesthetic capabilities and developed the model rooms as guides for people to copy in their own home. Just as in their approach to their sales catalogs, the Wrights stressed the functional and traditional character of the *American Way* line in its display and arrangement by geographic region so that each object's local

FIGURE 1.4 *Demonstration Room at R.H. Macy's for* American Way, *New York, c. 1940. (Russel Wright Papers, Syracuse University Libraries).*

roots would be clearly discernable. Unfortunately, even though the price of *American Way* items were kept affordable, the promotion and management of the program was far too complicated for the Wrights to orchestrate. Sales for the *American Way* line did not come up to projections, and the project was abandoned in 1942.

Guide to Easier Living

Exempted from military services because of his poor eyesight and age, Russel Wright spent his time during the Second World War working for the Red Cross and conducting extensive surveys on food service methods and housekeeping techniques. These studies along with earlier projects such as the *American Way* enabled the Wrights to formulate a master plan for modern American home design which they presented in their popular and widely influential book *Guide to Easier Living* (Figure 1.5). Published in 1950, the *Guide* provided the developing postwar society with blueprints for interiors that were suitable for a "new American way of life." As social commentator Russell Lynes points out, "Wright ... concerned himself with producing American Design that Americans could accept not because of any rigid doctrine of functionalism but because, to use a Quaker phrase, 'it spoke to their condition'" (Hennessey 1983: 11). In their book, the Wrights' expounded an approach to interior design that was based more on principles than on aesthetics. The *Guide* opens on its first page with the rhetorical question: "Do our homes really express the ideals of democracy and individualism we all profess?" (Wright 1950: 1). The Wrights then quickly argue that they do not and continue by pointing out that merely copying contemporary and historical styles undermines average Americans' ability to make choices and express themselves. "In this increasingly mechanized civilization, our homes are the one remaining place for personal expression, the place where we could really be ourselves," they state, "but in actuality they are more often than not undistinguished and without individuality, monuments to meaningless conformity" (Wright 1950).

Individualism was a key topic of the immediate postwar period and was viewed as a necessary part of revitalizing the economy and making America strong. Historian Arthur Schlesinger Jr. had summed up this postwar call for individualism in his 1949 book *The Vital Center*, when he claimed that the key issue facing the United States in the postwar period was not Soviet Communism but the "power of organizations over individuals" (Schlesinger 1949: 2). Schlesinger concluded that the successful future of the United States during the postwar years rested largely on a renewed sense of individual freedom and less on organizational control. Promoters of individualism campaigned that it was essential to the "American Way of Life" that was

FIGURE 1.5 *Window Display for* Guide to Easier Living, *16 East 34th Street, New York City, c. 1951. (Russel Wright Papers, Syracuse University Libraries)*

being promoted after the war, and set out to convince Americans of all ranks that free enterprise and the protection of individual rights would guarantee social harmony and abundance. Americans were encouraged to express their individualism through the purchase of consumer goods such as automobiles, home furnishing, and appliances and were offered a plethora of choices of colors and styling to support their personal expression.

One of the goals of the Wrights' *Guide* was to enable the American public to sort through those choices and purchase appropriately to imbue their homes with their own individualism by making choices based on good design principles. For the Wrights, good design meant choosing quality products. Whether they be American antiques or contemporary manufactured goods did not matter. It was more important that they be appropriately functional and suitable for the contemporary family's needs, and that well-chosen elements should work together in the design to create a life-enhancing and aesthetically pleasing environment. The Wrights' development of open stock furniture and dishware, for example, enabled consumers to pick and choose pieces from a wide variety of options in a particular line and encouraged them to assemble rooms expressive of their personal character as well as adaptable to their own particular needs and budgets. The freedom to make choices and thereby to express one's individuality within clearly prescribed and acceptable limits was unquestionably deemed "the American Way" by the Wrights and their distributors.

As much as the Wrights viewed America's historical past as the appropriate source for a particularly American brand of modern design, they did not believe that the direct replication of such styles was appropriate for contemporary homes. A recurrent theme in the *Guide to Easier Living* is that clinging to ideas of "the old Dream"—attempting to emulate the rich by copying traditional historical styles—was neither appropriate nor ultimately fulfilling. The Wrights point out, such aping of historical styles "saddled us with fussy homes, with a code of snobbish manners in a time of social change, with a dictatorship of etiquette that stifles individuality" (Wright 1950: 2). They insisted that if the American home was inadequate for contemporary living, its inadequacies "must be attributed primarily to a continued adherence to an ill-fitting and outmoded cultural pattern." They elaborated their solution to this problem:

> We believe the new American home will be a much simpler one to live in. Its size and its furnishings will be determined by the family's needs, not by arbitrary dictates of fashion. Living in it will be based on an informal and improvised design, rather than on a formal, traditional pattern. Its etiquette will derive from modern democratic ideals. (Wright 1950)

For the Wrights, the postwar American home constituted a participatory democracy, which resembled the American government's premise that everyone needed to play a role in its maintenance and development. Essential to this approach is the progressive idea that the whole family must participate in the maintenance of the home. The idea of democracy, not feminism, enabled the Wrights to conclude that the man of the house must do his equal share in house cleaning, food preparation, and child care. In their book, they rejected traditional gender roles: "Tradition needn't act as a stumbling block: The father may be the best interior decorator or pie baker, a daughter an incipient plumber" (Wright 1950: 136). The American man, they insisted, who "has learned to push a baby carriage with pride will also learn that it is not beneath his dignity to push a vacuum cleaner" (Wright 1950: 6). Children also were actively encouraged to be helpful around the house and were assigned numerous jobs from helping take care of younger siblings to cleaning up after themselves. In one democratic suggestion, the Wright's recommended that each member of the family be responsible for setting their own place at the table and clearing and washing their own dishes and silverware after the meal. Perhaps even more controversially, they suggested that dinner guests and partygoers in the house also contribute to the preparation and cleanup as part of a new participatory type of entertaining they called "the new hospitality." In one of their detailed and often humorous illustrations included in the book, a crowded group of partygoers is in the kitchen helping with the dishes. The caption reads, "Cleanup can even be a part of the evening's pleasure, if managed properly." This new kind of informality where everyone would be asked to participate was reportedly appalling to Emily Post, the contemporary arbiter of good manners. Hennessey reports that Post "attacked the very idea of informal service" and that Russel Wright responded in defense "with great gusto" (Hennessey 1991: 43). Emily Post's objections of course would have been considered derived from too much consideration of the "old Dream" and historically derived aristocratic models of manners.

The democratic ideal of "freedom" was also an important concept in the Wrights' approach to their interiors. To them, freedom not only meant the opportunity to make choices without being encumbered by rigid traditional approaches, but it also connoted a release from the drudgery of housework so that one might enjoy oneself and savor more fully the basic components of a truly democratic life. The Wrights' approach to creating freedom through interior design is an ideological as well as a functional one. Both Taylor and Ford served as models for them, and in their book they include an entire chapter on housework organization and Time-Motion studies. They begin this chapter entitled "Housewife-Engineer" by explaining: "We ... found that methods developed in industry are now being applied to the home. The drudgery of housework is now being attacked in a scientist-conducted revolution" (Wright 1950: 124). As Lindsay Stamm Shapiro suggests in "A Man and His Manners: Resetting the American Table," Russel and Mary Wright thoroughly embraced the time management of American industry and became "the Henry Fords of dinnerware and entertainment" (Albrecht et al. 2001: 25). In *Guide to Easier Living* the Wrights suggest that every activity in the house be scrutinized to discern how one can do it faster and easier. Detailed instructions and drawings are included that instruct readers in the most efficient way to make a bed, for example, and other regular housecleaning activities. To enhance ease and efficiency, the Wrights suggest that all upholstery should be able to be detached from the furniture and put in the washer. All furniture should be on casters or easy for anyone to move allowing choice and flexibility. New materials like Micarta, a first-generation plastic laminate, are suggested for use on tabletops and work surfaces because their durability and cleanability allowed a freedom of use: "You should be able to put a drink down anywhere without hunting for a coaster and feeling guilty," the authors recommend (Wright 1950: 20). Another one of the Wrights' functional time-saving recommendations that became a part of almost every postwar home was the pass-through window between the kitchen and dining room. The pass-through facilitated quick and easy transport of food into the dining room and dirty dishes back into the kitchen. A more developed version recommended by the Wrights is the dutch-door type pass-through that opens to allow an entire table to roll in and out of the kitchen for setting and clearing.

The *Guide to Easier Living* is filled with "how-to" lists, helpful tips, and illustrative drawings that detail specific examples. For the most part the overall aesthetic as well as the types of furniture shown in the drawings are simple and insistently modern and include current products designed and manufactured in the United States by Ray and Charles Eames, George Nelson, and Eero Saarinen. Never missing an opportunity for self-promotion, however, the Wrights also included their own line of *Easier Living* furniture, which embodied all of their recommendations. In 1950, Stratton Furniture Company produced this group of fifty pieces designed by Russel Wright. Like the earlier *American Modern* furniture, the *Easy Living* group was constructed of solid wood in a blonde finish and had references back to solid furniture of the colonial period. However, unlike the earlier series, the new pieces exhibited a more pronounced flexibility and functionality. The lounge chair and sofa were designed with an arm on one end, which folded up as a table and then folded out on the other end to make a magazine rack. The coffee table had a sliding top that revealed an inset porcelain tray inside to hold food and beverages. The magazine stand was on casters for easy movement. Slipcovers snapped on and off for easy cleaning, and the night table had pull-out shelves, which extended over the bed for reading or eating.

The dynamism of this furniture illustrates perhaps the most interesting and insightful characteristic the Wrights identified in their approach to a distinctly American interior design: an openness to change and flexibility. The Wrights viewed the United States as a dynamic culture, based more on the idea of constant change than the more static notion of an invariant identity. To be American was to embrace the energy and dynamics of change. The Wrights believed that the interior therefore should not be a static and inflexible environment but a vital, moving, and evolving one. Their book is filled with

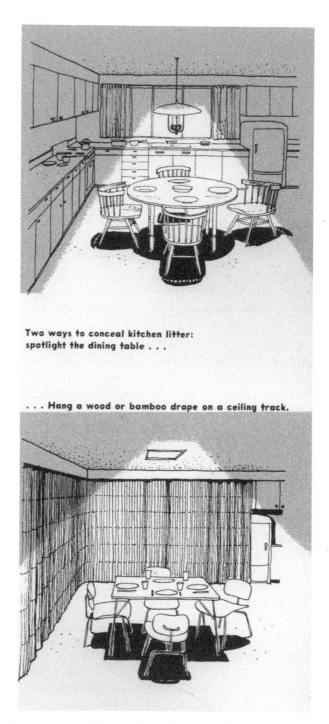

FIGURE 1.6 *Illustration of Kitchen Transformation from* Guide to Easier Living, *1950. (Russel Wright Papers, Syracuse University Libraries).*

alternative scenarios, where a given room or the entire house can be used in one way for a special event or particular time of day, and then inhabited in yet another manner at another time. They show how a kitchen, for example, can be transformed into a romantic sophisticated dining room by drawing a curtain around all the kitchen cabinets and appliances and modulating the lighting scheme. Various techniques to make these kinds of transformations are illustrated in the book (Figure 1.6).

This concept of changeability was probably most notably implemented in the Wrights' design of their own retirement house, Dragon Rock, located north of New York City in Garrison, New York. At Dragon Rock, which was sited to interact as much as possible with its Edenic natural setting, the interior finishes were designed to change with the seasons. It reportedly took the three occupants of the house three days to make the seasonal changes throughout the building (Albrecht et al. 2001: 116). In the summer, window coverings were made out of white yarn, while in winter they were composed of bands of warm red ribbon. Cabinet doors were double-faced so that they were cool white Formica in summer and warm Indian Red in the winter. In addition, the wall panel in the dining room, which consisted of white film and fiberglass in the summer was changed to a bronze sheet metal surface in the winter. Wright also devised seasonally appropriate alternatives for the upholstery and rugs.

While the *Guide to Easier Living* codified and collected the Wrights' ideas for creating a specifically American approach to interior design, the Wright residences in New York City, realized before the book's publication, served as the laboratories and case studies for the ideas promoted in their book. In 1937, the Wrights moved to a new penthouse in the Concord Apartments at 130 East 40th Street. Furnished in metal tubular furnishings, gooseneck lamps, a sofa with a cantilevered table of Russel Wright design, this interior was one of first of many showroom/houses the Wright family was to occupy. Within its overall elegant and simplified modern styling, the Wrights incorporated new American technologies and materials such as rubber-tiled floor, pre-manufactured glass walls and glass block. The dining room table, which exhibited the flexibility and ease of care promoted later by the *Guide*, was covered with an easily cleanable Formica surface, and could be folded up and converted into a display stand and an easel for presentations to clients. In a conference room for his home/office in the late 1940s, Wright incorporated the same multi-functional kind of table. The *Interiors* magazine review of new work in the summer of 1949 noted this feature:

Focal point in Mr. Wright's new conference and display room is the black Formica table, which does tricks. It can expand to twice its normal width, for large displays, and it can rise up and tilt in three positions to make a sort of easel to show drawings and photographs. (*Interiors* 109 August 1949: 101)

In that same space, Wright also specified that the chartreuse green upholstery of the sofa should be woven out of aluminum, plexon, and saran, and that the curtains be made of a semi-transparent white fabric coated with vinylite, all new materials that made the surfaces they covered both durable and cleanable. This contributed to the "freedom from drudgery" and ease of maintenance that was also promoted by the Wrights. The Wrights also included in these projects Russel's Cowboy Modern chair, which combines a sense of American rustic history and craftsmanship with modern styling. Together with animal skins used as rugs and some neoclassical style furniture in the interior, they soften the design's strict geometric modernity and suggest a sense of a longer history or tradition by successfully linking the past and future tenses of American culture in the room's overall design. This relaxed, eclectic, functional approach is also evident in the Wrights' penthouse apartment at 7 Park Avenue in New York where they moved in 1942. Within it, their sleeping quarters were situated on the first floor, living room on the second, and a balcony/office on the third floor. The design of this apartment highlighted more organic materials and shapes and the walls comprised simple square panels with no embellishment except the wood grain pattern marking each piece. A gently curving upholstered sofa echoes the organicism of the *American Modern* dishware. Design historian and Wright scholar Donald Albrecht observes: "Warmer and more hospitable than the previous residence in the Concord, the Park Avenue apartment suggested the move toward the casual and gracious postwar concept of 'easier living'" (Albrecht et al. 2001: 102).

Some of the same features distinguishing their apartments are repeated in their speculative design for a modern house illustrated in their *Better Homes and Gardens* article entitled "How Will You Live Tomorrow?" published in 1944. Floor to ceiling wood paneling similar to that in the Park Avenue apartment line the wall as doors to storage cabinets which house dishes, glassware, games, and other entertainment paraphernalia. A full-paneled glass window wall links the outdoor patio with the indoors and can be slid entirely open to join the two spaces. Two Cowboy Modern chairs, a curvilinear sofa, and an animal skin rug soften the geometric lines of the space. In addition, the stone fireplace, unadorned by a mantelpiece, projects the ambience of an American rustic traditional space. A low freestanding partition between the living room and the work area allows a flow of activities and light between the two spaces. In the center of a built-in storage wall, the ubiquitous and functional pass-through is incorporated to connect the dining and kitchen areas. Their ideas for open, more informal multi-purpose spaces demonstrated here, which are extremely functional yet flexible and therefore more appropriate for the contemporary American lifestyle, are highlighted in their *Guide to Easier Living* and are fully implemented in this scheme.

After the war, the Wrights moved into four-story brownstone at 221 East 48th Street that became their permanent home until Russel Wright moved to Dragon Rock after Mary's death in 1952. The building contained their own living and office space as well as two separate rental units. Once again, the house was a "real-life laboratory for testing ideas for *Guide to Easier Living*" (Albrecht et al. 2001: 104). A September 1949 article in *Interiors* magazine featured the Wrights' new home and noted such typical Wright features as the glass-paneled pass-through that separated the dining room and kitchen, the storage wall and desk in the living room similar to the Park Avenue apartment. The window blind in this room served a double function as a projection screen, and the furniture in the space rested on casters for easy rearranging. The *Interiors* article pointed out that on the street level of the Wrights' work space, "it is difficult to find a single non-functional object" and that "the conference room is an ideal machine for display" (*Interiors* 109 September, 1949: 89). A curvilinear-shaped studio space, which was added on to the first floor by Wright, is noted as being "as handsome as Russel Wright's justly famous dinnerware—and as sensible." A continuous row of six-foot windows along its curving wall lets in light and allows an open view of the patio garden, giving the space a sense of expansiveness that was enhanced by a brilliant lemon-yellow paint on its ceiling. Everything in the studio space was made or covered in materials that could be wiped off with a damp cloth, including the curtains, which were made of white, semi-transparent vinyl. In the living spaces, the Wrights explored the same utility and durability. Cost-effective and long-lasting fluorescent tubes are placed in the bookshelves to illuminate their contents. The cushions on the sofa are constructed of easy-to-clean black-and-white nylon. The coffee table has a removable glass top. And the storage wall and kitchen area are concealed by a flexible wood-weave partition. At the same time the Wrights softened the space with their interjection of more traditional or historically referential materials that are specifically American. The Cowboy Modern chairs and animal skin rugs appear again. The brick of the walls is left exposed in some areas and interacts with the soapstone used to make the fireplace. In a nod to American individuality, Mary Wright's bedroom is appointed in Victorian details and furniture. The article notes the richness such eclecticism and diversity brings to the space: "Perhaps they decided that it would be stimulating and not at all unpleasant to step from the Hardoy chair and raised fireplace of the living room, into a quaint bedroom (Mary Wright's) where festoons of Nottingham lace dyed solid pink adorn the windows" (Albrecht et al. 2001: 91). As a result of the Wrights' hybrid functionalist approach, the overall impact of the space is described as "poetic" with the proviso:

The house is already unusually interesting, not only because it works well, but because its design, though unpretentious, exerts an oddly poignant emotional appeal. Using simple—almost ordinary—elements and without straining for effect the Wrights have produced a very lovely space ... Too often, the word "modern" in interior design implies a negative process ... stripping, removing ... What makes this house so successful, however, is what he added to it. (Albrecht et al. 2001: 89)

In the 48th Street House, the Wrights were successful in creating what is described in detail in *Guide to Easier Living* as "another kind of beauty ... found in informal design," that is "an apt expression of our own times" and as the Wrights would argue an appropriately American kind of experience (Wright 1950: 8). This approach to interior design was brought to its ultimate expression in the Wright house in Garrison, New York, built in the 1950s. At Dragon Rock, Wright created his best example of modern design derived from American traditions that is both functional and life enhancing as well as appropriate for the "new American way of life." The Wrights bought the property in Garrison in 1942 with the idea of creating a getaway from the stresses of New York City and the business world. In his 1961 lecture, "The Home as a Personal Statement," Russel Wright explained the need to create such a place:

As the assembly line encroaches more and more on our working life, crowding out individual creative expression, the need for a home in which we can realize ourselves as individuals become increasingly urgent. My own experimental and personal country home is intended as an experiment and demonstration that contemporary design can create from old and new materials a home that is individual, capable of the variety of moods that can be found in traditional homes, a home that can join the emotional, sentimental and aesthetic characteristics with the practicality and comfort that we have created in the 20th century. (Wright 2001: 63)

Sited on the edge of an abandoned and flooded quarry, Dragon Rock contains many of the Wrights' typical functional "American know-how" kind of innovations. In the kitchen, a counterbalanced shelf for storing glassware can be pushed up into the ceiling over the buffet counter. A silver drawer in this same counter opens into both the kitchen and the dining areas. A dumbwaiter connects the front hall with a special shelf near the refrigerator. As outlined in their *Guide,* the house is a textbook on the Wrights' brand of American functionalism, including their now typical vocabulary of durable easy-to-clean materials and a mix of modern, historical, and natural details. Built-in cabinets clad in Formica are placed adjacent to natural stone floors from the quarry. Synthetic durable fabrics of nylon, resin, and Plexiglas are mixed with tree trunks, which are employed as beams and wall panels with pressed grasses and flowers in them. The house testifies to how old and new, as well as natural and manmade, can be combined in an unmistakably contemporary setting that takes the greatest advantage of both, but is also clearly appropriate to its time, specific context, and the individualism of its inhabitants. As outlined earlier, the house is able to change with the seasons, reflecting a sense of vitality and change so important to the Wrights. But even more importantly in this house, Russel Wright is intent on evoking an appreciation of the rugged beauty of nature. Donald Albrecht posits that "Dragon Rock and Manitoga's (the name of the grounds) relationship with its environment represented Wright's belief that contemporary Americans must seek to live in harmony with nature" (Albrecht et al. 2001: 119). Following the tradition of landscape designer Frederick Law Olmsted and the Hudson River painters, Wright molded both the house and the site to create a romanticized and celebratory view of nature. The design of the house and the site are inseparable and work together to create a theatrical experience. Approaching the house one can hear a waterfall but cannot see it; this absence creates a sense of anticipation. An entryway on a small landing passes down a set of wooden steps to an open living area that functions as a theater from which one can view nature. The room is constructed of a natural slate floor, a large corner fireplace made of boulders for the nearby quarry, which also create a long curving staircase that leads to the dining and kitchen. A typical Russel Wright low counter divides the dining area from the kitchen. The dining room and seating areas curve gently to embrace the view of the stone patios and quarry through the full height glass walls. The main living area connects with two other areas: a studio/bedroom for Russel, and the living/ bedroom area for his daughter, Ann, and her governess. These three main areas were connected by vine-covered loggias, and each room includes its own private terrace. Ann Wright's bedroom was furnished with an assortment of Colonial, Victorian, and Modern elements and includes an adjacent bathroom featuring a sunken blue-glass tile tub with miniature hot and cold waterfalls and a private terrace with an outdoor fireplace. In spring of 1962, *Life* magazine ran a feature on Dragon Rock in which it is referred to as "an enchanted world in the woods framed in comfort and beauty" (*Life*, March 16, 1962: 74–83). Today it is open to visitors as an instructional model of the Wrights' particular version of American modern home. The house and the property are owned and operated by the Russel Wright Design Center, a private non-profit organization, and was named a National Historic Landmark in 2006, giving it an official designation as specifically significant American home.

The Wrights' legacy

Historians and critics of modern design in the postwar period tend to be mixed in their opinions on the interiors of Russel and Mary Wright and their zealously American approach. As early as the 1950s, the Wrights' idea of

"Easier Living" was being debunked. In 1951, The *New Yorker* criticized their book, proclaiming:

> It is doubtful whether the new life differs very much—except in being more self-conscious and less pleasing—from that led by most young Americans of the present day … Under household management, the modern ways of doing things advocated by the Wrights … may make many readers wonder if they haven't, quite unconsciously, been leading the easy life all along. (Hennessey 1991: 53)

Biographer William Hennessey also pointed out the dubious merit of the Wrights' ideas, particularly in interior design concepts developed in Russel Wright's later years, claiming that his work grew from "a design experiment to an obsession" and created an overly controlled and rationalized way of life instead of being the hallmark of individuality and freedom he claimed:

> As happened so often in Wright's life, his penchant for machine-like domestic efficiency seemed, paradoxically, to make life more complex and inflexible. Instead of the "informality" he so professed, Wright had succeeded in creating a new sort of formality that expressed his own personality and infuriated those around him. (Hennessey 1991: 76)

Wright was aware of this problem but considered it more a result of a cultural shift or a misunderstanding rather than a flaw of his theories. In a speech to the Society of Industrial Designers in 1976, the same year that he died, he stated:

> About 1953, "contemporary" began to be defeated. My religion, which I had pioneered for twenty years, was losing. I wanted to convert the masses–to design for middle and lower-class Americans a way of life expressive of what I thought was basic American taste. Now with postwar affluence … Easier Living, my book and design group had failed. (Hennessey 1991: 65)

Regardless of his own sense of failure, Wright's theories had an indelible impact on interior design and the effort to create a particularly American design sensibility. His contemporary George Nelson was quoted in the obituary written for him by the *New York Times* that he was the person most responsible for "the shift in taste toward modern in the late 1930s"(Reif, *New York Times*, December 23, 1976). In their interiors and *Guide to Easier Living*, Russel and Mary Wright re-conceptualized the design of the American home and created a new model of living that embodied the flexibility, informality, and practicality of a distinctly American approach to interior design, which lent both validity and a sense of tradition to this emerging American practice. Critiques of the Wrights' sensibilities and their, at times, overly zealous approach to creating a national style cannot undermine their long-lasting impact on design as well as their sincere desire to give their fellow citizens appropriately American design. As magazine editor Julia Johnson points out in her praise for Wright's work in 1992:

> Wright's designs were refreshing, pared down, practical, and affordable, for the informal way he imagined American men and women wanted to live. (Wright 2001: 42)

Parts of this chapter were first published in Lucinda Kaukas Havenhand (2014) "Russel and Mary Wright's *Guide to Easier Living* and the 'New American Way of Life,'" *Interiors*, 5:2, 199–218 and are reused here with permission of Taylor and Francis Group: https://www.tandfonline.com/10.2752/20419121 4X14038639021207

2

Richard Neutra and the Therapeutic Interior

Our understanding of Richard Neutra's interiors may be best known through the iconic photographs taken by photographer Julius Shulman of buildings like the Kaufmann House in Palm Springs, which document the clean white walls, extensive windows, and exquisite siting in natural settings of the houses he is known for (Figure 2.1). In many ways the images of the houses with their drama and classical elegance have become the stereotype for what modern domestic architecture was and could be in the United States. Movies like *LA Confidential*, which used Neutra's Lovell house as a set, and other popular culture and advertising use of their imagery made them a standard device to portray the ideas of modern wealth, power, sophistication, and glamour. The *raison d'être* in their concept and development, however, was far from that purpose. Richard Neutra, unlike many architects and designers of his time, was less concerned with the aesthetics of the house and its emblematic modernist sensibilities than with how it could accommodate and enhance the lifestyles of its occupants and promote a healthy and life-enriching experience. Although generally identified as a disseminator of the International Style in America, Neutra always maintained strong social and behavioral concerns in his work that were far different than that movement's basic tenets. His wife Dione Neutra noted this in her introduction to a collection of her husband's essays published in 1989:

> Over the years, almost all of the historians, critics, and various other reviewers have emphasized Richard's "style," whereas his interest was in well-being of the people who came to him, the health and happiness of society generally, and the relationship of his designs to the contours and elements of nature … He was a devoutly responsible experimenter who, had he tried to cater to the prevalent taste, would have felt and immobilizing disgust with himself. (Marlin 1989: xxi)

FIGURE 2.1 *Richard Neutra, Kaufmann House, Palm Springs, 1947. (© J. Paul Getty Trust. Getty Research Institute, Los Angeles, 2004.R.10. Photo: Julius Shulman).*

Influenced by the work of architect Frank Lloyd Wright and psychologists Sigmund Freud, Wilhelm Wundt, and Wilhelm Reich, Richard Neutra developed a personal and unique approach to interior design call "bio-realism," which mixed the study of biology, physiology, psychology, current popular theories of health and medicine as well as his own philosophy to create what he deemed would be the most life-enhancing and healthy environments for his clients. An exploration of the origins, development, and application of Neutra's theories reveals how they shaped his brand of modernism, particularly the "therapeutic" domestic interiors he created in the United States from the late 1920s into the 1960s.

Vienna, Europe, and dreams of America

With a career that spanned from 1915 to 1970, Neutra biographer Thomas Hines reflects: "His work, his life experience, his search for modern architecture coincided neatly with the larger movement's life frame ... he experienced the buoyant struggles of modernism's early years, the heady success of its mid-century ascendancy, and the perplexing strains of its slow demise" (Hines 1982: 4). Richard Neutra was born in Vienna, the capital of the Austro-Hungarian Empire in 1892, as the son of a machinist/foundry owner. He experienced childhood during a culturally rich period when the city was at the peak of its position as a center for creative and intellectual inquiry and was populated with such noteworthy individuals as Sigmund Freud, the musicians Arnold Schönberg and Gustav Mahler, artists Gustav Klimt and Egon Schiele, and architects Adolf Loos and Otto Wagner, as well as many other *fin-de-siècle* luminaries who were focused on investigating modern life in their work. He was a schoolmate and life-long friend of Ernst Freud, son of the famous psychoanalyst, and was a frequent visitor to their home. Neutra had a personal relationship with Sigmund Freud and continuously consulted him concerning the treatment of their son Frank, who was born with an intellectual developmental disorder. Both this experience as well as his childhood familiarity with the famous psychologist contributed to Neutra's keeping abreast of Freud's writings and theories throughout his lifetime.

In 1911 Neutra entered a four-year program in architecture at the Vienna Technische Hochschule. During his second year, he began to attend the studio/salon of architect Adolf Loos, where he was exposed to his ideas about modernism and met fellow student and future collaborator Rudolf Schindler. Both Schindler and Neutra were greatly influenced by Loos's enthusiasm for modern design and American culture. Through Loos, they became enamored with the work of Frank Lloyd Wright and made a pact to "go to the places where he walked and worked" (Drexler and Hines 1982: 5). Schindler fulfilled this commitment first, leaving for the United States in 1914. Neutra planned to follow soon after but was called for active military duty when the First World War broke out. He served as an artillery lieutenant in Serbia and contracted malaria and tuberculosis during the first years of the war. His illness prevented him from continuing his military duties and he was hospitalized in 1916, entering into a period of infirmity and recuperation that lasted over two years. In his memoir *Life and Shape*, he recalled that he was in eighteen different hospitals "in as many months" as he was slowly transported away from the war zone toward home. After the war in 1919, Neutra moved to Stäfa, Switzerland, near Zurich to continue his recovery in a rest home. He attended classes taught by the architect Karl Moser in Zurich and continued to develop his skills as an architect and draftsman. Through his acquaintance with Regula Niedermann, also a resident of the rest home, he met Dione Niedermann, her sister and his future wife.

Neutra began his career as an architect soon after meeting Dione in 1920 and worked in Switzerland and Germany, finding positions in various offices, most notably in Berlin in the office of Eric Mendelsohn, the prominent expressionist modernist. Letters from Schindler describing the moderate California climate and his work for Frank Lloyd Wright inspired Neutra to leave Germany and work toward emigrating to the United States. Neutra was desperate to leave Europe and wrote in a letter to Schindler, "If only I could get to the United States! How I wish I could!" He reports that to keep himself going during the time he lived and worked in Switzerland, dealing with a poor-paying job, bitterly cold winter, depression, and his painful memories of the recent war years he "repeated inwardly 'California calls you,'" a slogan he had seen on an advertisement sign in Zurich. "I kept it in my heart as suggestive formulation thinking. What one wishes ardently has to be repeated in a pregnant sentence and ever so often repeated over and over again" (D. Neutra 1986: 7). In 1922, he married Dione Niedermann and in 1923 fulfilled his wish to emigrate to the United States and departed for New York City, leaving his new wife behind to await the birth of their first child. The decision to separate from his wife and expected child was a difficult one for them both but motivated by the deteriorating conditions in Germany. "It appears to me that it is high time to leave this district of humanity," Neutra wrote to Frances Toplitz from Berlin, "during the last days, we lost again, for the hundredth time, half of our savings without being horrified" (D. Neutra 1986: 94). He settled in New York for a short time after he arrived in the United States where he was pleased to report to his wife that he would be making $35.00 a week. But Neutra found the new experience and environment, from dealing with language difference, the density, and diversity of the city itself as well as the things he found strange, such as having "no spot that corresponds to our cafes," difficult and uncomfortable (D. Neutra: 100). He soon migrated to Chicago where he found work with the noted architecture firm of Holabird and Roche. In Chicago, he visited buildings in the vicinity that were designed by Louis Sullivan and Wright and met Sullivan in 1924 and Wright at Sullivan's funeral soon thereafter. Seeing Wright's work was inspiring to him but in his comments to Dione about it he hints of his developing concern about how architecture should work to positively shape the humans who live in it. "I have seen some of Wright's work," he wrote, "However the people who live in these houses were rather awful. I had always hoped that the new architecture would produce a different human being" (D. Neutra: 120). Dione Neutra and their new son (named Frank Lloyd in honor of the master architect) joined her husband in June 1924. They were invited by Wright to stay at Taliesin, his home in Wisconsin, as his guests, students, and employees. Dione Neutra noted in her diary that their stay there was "like a dream" and one of the most idyllic times of their lives (Hines 1982: 54). Neutra worked for Wright for about a year; then in 1925 he made his move to Los Angeles to join Schindler who had moved there permanently when he worked on Wright's house for Aline Barnsdall.

"California calls you"

Neutra began his architectural career in California, living and working with Rudolf Schindler. Schindler and his wife Pauline attracted a number of progressive thinkers, artists, and writers to their home for their frequent parties and salons. Dione Neutra described the arrangement in a letter from 1925:

> Schindler awaited us in Los Angeles and brought us to his strange house in Hollywood, which has its own beauty considering how little money he has. We live in the guest apartment, have a large room with kitchen and bath and a separate entrance. Mrs. Schindler is extraordinarily helpful and both of them show great friendship and help us a lot ... Schindler told Richard that he feels a sentimental attachment to him and considers our two families as a "unit." Whether they should later collaborate remains to be seen. (D. Neutra 1986: 136)

Neutra and Schindler did collaborate on an entry for the 1926 League of Nations competition and formed the Architectural Group for Industry and Commerce together, but their partnership was short-lived. Although the two couples enjoyed a communal life of intellectual and cultural exchange at first, relations between the Neutras and Schindlers became strained beyond repair by 1927, when Philip and Leah Lovell bypassed Schindler, who had designed their famous house at Newport Beach in 1926, to award the commission to build their new house in Los Angeles to Neutra. Schindler later claimed that Neutra stole the Lovell's Los Angeles commission from him, creating bad feelings between the two men that were only reconciled toward the end of both their lives, when on the occasion of Neutra's second heart attack he was randomly assigned to a double room whose other occupant was none other than Schindler. The two had rarely spoken to each other in twenty years but were able to re-establish their friendship because of this chance experience. The Neutras shared both a home and social activities with the Schindlers until they left for a year trip to Europe and Asia in 1930 and then they went their separate ways.

    The completion of the new Lovell House in 1929 brought fame and recognition to Neutra and established his reputation as a modern architect of note in the United States. His modernist stance was enriched by his 1930 trip to Europe, Japan, and China where he spent time with prominent designers Alvar Aalto, Walter Gropius, Le Corbusier, and Mies van der Rohe as well as a month teaching at the Bauhaus as a visiting critic. During his time in Holland he also met C.H. Van der Leeuw, a Dutch industrialist, who arranged for him to stay at the recently completed Schroeder House designed by Gerrit Rietveld. Van der Leeuw shared many interests in design and technology with Neutra and supported him morally and sometimes financially throughout his career, lending him the money to build his own first home. Dione Neutra wrote excitedly about this to her parents:

> Finally, the miracle has occurred, most wonderful news. A patron has loaned us money so the Richard may demonstrate in a small house what kind of progressive materials are available price wise, and that such a small dwelling need not be "uncomfortable" or have a "hospital-like" atmosphere. In this manner, we will acquire a house an office designed by Richard where he can demonstrate his ideas. (D. Neutra 1986: 227)

On returning to Los Angeles in 1931 Neutra established his own home and studio and took on as apprentices Gregory Ain, Harwell Harris, and Raphael Soriano (who all became notable California architects). In 1932 Neutra was featured along with Le Corbusier, Gropius, Mies, and Wright in the pivotal *Modern Architecture* show at the Museum of Modern Art for which curators Philip Johnson and Henry Russell Hitchcock coined the label "International Style." At this time, Museum of Modern Art Director Alfred Barr referred to Neutra as second only to Wright in his international reputation (Hines 1982: 251).

In the 1930s Neutra designed many houses that allowed him to develop a signature style. In his projects that range from small bungalows to large mansions for movie stars and members of high society, Neutra translated the vocabulary of International Style modern to meet the needs of West Coast living. Although each house and interior are unique, Neutra's '30s houses all employ a similar design vocabulary. The primary structure for each is a strong horizontal pavilion or pavilions with light vertical members. These pavilions are generally closed on one side and open on the other with bands of windows and sliding glass doors. The roofs are consistently flat (except in the rare cases when building codes dictated a pitched roof) with cantilevered overhangs that partially shade the expanses of glass. The closed side of the building sometimes exhibited a high clerestory window, depending on the arrangement of the building on the site. His buildings of this period exhibit a lightness, thinness, and simplicity that make them visually rich and elegant. Wood framing, inside and out, was generally painted to look like metal to emphasize the machine-like character of the designs. This machine aesthetic was often reinforced by the use of metal siding, glass block, and other industrial and prefabricated materials (Figure 2.2).

In his 1930s houses Neutra continuously demonstrated his interest in harnessing new technologies for the purpose of good design. In this early

FIGURE 2.2 *Richard Neutra, Miller "Mensendieck" House, 1937. (© J. Paul Getty Trust. Getty Research Institute, Los Angeles, 2004.R.10. Photo: Julius Shulman).*

work, Neutra, like most European modernists, was convinced that technology directed the path that design must take. In 1929, he had stated in *Architectural Record*, "Since materials determine building modes, and since industrial conditions affect materials, it is clear that industry determines architectural styles." He was an avid reader and researcher and like the Wrights was also greatly influenced by the time-motion studies and efficiency theories developed by Henry Ford and Frederick Winslow Taylor. He found in their speculations possibilities for creating a mass-produced, industrialized model of building:

> A European might think that this enormous market should offer the possibility of enhancing opportunities for research and development, which would in turn lead to a profitable growth of the industry, and in particular of the field of construction. [...] Only modern architecture can actually benefit from this, as it not only possesses the ingenuousness and the machinery required to produce new prefabricated pieces but, above all, has the mechanisms for distribution [...] including prefabricated houses commissioned in return, as well as the methods to control them. (Neutra 1962: 190)

Neutra wrote about this approach specifically in his first two books: *Wie baut Amerika* (1927) and *Amerika: Die Stilbildung des Neuen Bauens in den Vereingten Staaten* (1930). His own home of 1932, built with a loan from C.H. Van der Leeuw, which he called the V.D.L. Research House in his honor, was a testing ground for his study of materials and standardization. His work on the V.D.L. House enabled him to establish the vocabulary he would use in his other houses of the '30s, which varied in size and location from the intimate less-than-1200-square-foot space of his house for Grace Lewis Miller in the desert at Palm Springs in 1937 to his sprawling estate for John Nicholas Brown on Fishers Island, New York, in 1938. Each of these designs allowed him to experiment with different technological innovations. Some houses incorporated radiant floors while others were notable for self-cooling exterior walls that controlled interior temperatures. Some had large overhangs that provided built-in light and heat control. Screened soffits and sliding doors were strategically placed in the houses to provide ventilation. Pools were added not only for aesthetics and recreation but to provide moisture and moderate interior temperatures. Neutra explored easily maintained prefabricated materials and components illustrated in the Sweet's catalogs, which became the source of inspiration for many of his buildings.[1] In his house for Charles Richter, the developer of the Richter scale, Neutra integrated some of the first attempts at earthquake-proof engineering. Lighting was also an important aspect of his designs. His interiors were always designed to maximize the use of daylight while reducing the negative impact of glare and heat gain. Recessed lighting was often incorporated, and Neutra developed a trademark soffit lighting for the outside of his houses that illuminated the windows at night, making them appear opaque and hard to see through. This eliminated the reflection of the interior back onto the occupant in the mirroring of the plate glass windows and doors, a term he called "phantomic extension."

Neutra's interiors also emphasized flexibility and functionality, but not at the expense of the overall aesthetic. In plan his houses were consistently constructed of clusters of smaller units that could serve the varying needs of their occupants. Custom-designed furniture often contributed to the flexibility. A multiuse space, for example, may have a table that folded down over a washtub to make a breakfast room. The "Camel" table for Kahn House (1940) had legs that folded like a camel so that it could transform from a dining to a coffee table. Movable walls allowed small intimate spaces, used for private functions, to be expanded and combined with other spaces for public and social use. This flexibility was emphasized by Neutra's frequent use of large plate mirrors that doubled the volumes of the spaces and expanded the inner view in the same way the large windows expanded the outward view. Flexibility and expandability were key elements of Neutra's houses. Grace Miller referred to her home in Palm Springs, which exhibited all these characteristics, as a "smart house" that "lends itself easily for any kind of life" (Hines 1982: 121, note 16). Although exploring materiality and technology, Neutra never lost sight of the importance of the human experience in these houses:

> One of the principles of engineering honestly is not to torture materials, maltreat and force them in to forms and functions foreign to them. The supreme commandment, however should be not to torture human beings, the most precious materials daily trusted into our hands and to respect their subtle strains and stresses. Only if *they* are kept functioning right is the design functional—is it human. (Neutra 1962: 241)

While the early houses aspire to be more "machine-like" rather than "organic" in their appearance, they nonetheless share Neutra's concern, perhaps inherited from the work of Frank Lloyd Wright, for incorporating nature with them. The integration of indoors and outdoors was always a prime feature in Neutra houses, and roof decks, patios, and sleeping porches were liberally included in the designs. In addition, the natural qualities of sites were emphasized by

FIGURE 2.3 *Richard Neutra, Interior and Patio of V.D.L. Research House I, 1937. (© J. Paul Getty Trust. Getty Research Institute, Los Angeles, 2004.R.10. Photo: Julius Shulman).*

terraces, plantings, and landscaping (Figure 2.3). This is perhaps also inspired by his early training with the noted landscape designer Gustav Ammann, who Neutra apprenticed with in Switzerland and introduced him to the knowledge of plants, trees, and site landscaping. This experience gave him a foundation for his later theories of bio-realism if not inspiration for it. "I especially cherished watching the natural equilibria of the plant ecology and the generative microclimate of a site. Why not care equally for humans in their growth and biodynamics, I began to think. Why care less for *their* roots and blooms?" he wrote in *Life and Shape* (Neutra 1962: 138). Neutra's diaries and memoirs are filled with descriptions of his own experience with nature. "I go among books, if I cannot go among trees," he related in one of his late essays. Living in and with, observing and modeling from nature were life-long preoccupations of Neutra that he believed enhance the human experience and were reflected in his approach to all his work and labeled by him as "nature near".

The large expanse of glass and sliding doors he inserted into the design of these early houses reflected that interest and concern. In Neutra's interiors the "nature near" effect was reinforced by his use of long, low, horizontal built-in furniture that not only controlled the strict geometric compositions

FIGURE 2.4 *Richard Neutra, Interior, Marshall House, 1952. (© J. Paul Getty Trust. Getty Research Institute, Los Angeles, 2004.R.10. Photo: Julius Shulman).*

of the rooms but also framed rather than obstructed the large expanse of glass and the view and sense of space beyond (Figure 2.4). As architectural historian Stephen Leet points out in his monograph on the Miller House: "The configuration of low perimeter seating and casement windows emphasizes the psychological difference between foreground and distant view, between the shelter of the house and the landscape beyond, with a stepped progression from seating, to window sill to desert horizon" (Leet 2004: 109). The use of butt glazing and the minimal use or omission of intermediate window mullions added to this effect. Neutra's prominent use of sliding glass doors and screening added a sense of transparency between indoor and outdoor spaces, and in his interiors the outdoors generally always became part of the indoor room. These immediate exterior spaces were usually highly landscaped to work as an extension of the interior spaces and often exhibited features that extend between both, and stretched from the exterior through a glass wall into the interior space as in the Miller house. This ambiguous boundary between indoors and outdoors added to the comfort and delight of the interior space (Figure 2.5).

FIGURE 2.5 *Richard Neutra, Interior, Miller "Mensendieck" House, 1937. (© J. Paul Getty Trust. Getty Research Institute, Los Angeles, 2004.R.10. Photo: Julius Shulman).*

Shifting focus

By the 1940s and '50s, most authors agree that Neutra's view of and enthusiasm for technology had changed. *Time* magazine, which featured him on its cover in 1949, noted how Neutra had turned away from the "hard and cold" approach of the International Style to "softer and warmer forms and materials," by creating spaces that merged "clean lines, common-sense convenience and liberating openness of style with the warm overtones of home" (Hines 1982: 220). Hines notes that this tendency, which can be seen in Neutra's Nesbitt House of 1942 and Tremaine House of 1948, "struck an important nerve in regard to the needs and perceptions of the architectural public" (Hines 1982: 205). Although he continued to use industrialized materials in combination with a warmer palette of wood, brick, and textiles, these were less a stylistic change or concern for materials per se, but more a reflection of him giving more and more focus to a theme that consistently informed his work—the idea of creating therapeutic interiors (Figure 2.6). Neutra had always been interested in creating healthy and life-enhancing space but by the late '30s and '40s this focus developed into a passion that enveloped

FIGURE 2.6 *Richard Neutra, Interior, Nash House, 1957. (© J. Paul Getty Trust. Getty Research Institute, Los Angeles, 2004.R.10. Photo: Julius Shulman).*

and replaced his pre–Second World War interest in technology and building materials. This developing obsession was formulated into a theory he called "bio-realism." According to Leet, bio-realism was "a psycho-physiological philosophy" devised by Neutra "that attempted to weave theories from biological sciences into a therapeutic unity of harmonious surroundings" (Leet 2004: 172). Neutra believed that the rapid changes brought by industrialization had wreaked havoc on civilization, but these ill effects could be tempered by "ever better biological fitness of design" (Neutra 1954: 63). William Marlin in his introduction to his edited volume of Neutra's late essays posited that "the main message of Neutra's philosophy of bio-realism is that human beings have certain deep-seated needs, and that we had better know what they are—physiologically, psychologically, and in terms of their sensory and spiritual constitution" (Marlin 1989: viii). Neutra in his typical grandiose and expansive prose defined bio-realism himself as "the most practical sort of realism, taking in everything that is the body and soul of man—along with that space we call the psyche, which performs as a dynamic mediator between them ... The reality of the building was the space within ... this reality was the space within us—not just within our buildings" (Marlin 1989: xxii). In simplest terms, Neutra viewed the disharmonious state of the world as a crisis and believed that designers could not afford to make decisions based on the mere use of technology or functionalism but must consider the physiological and psychological impact of their creations. Neutra identifies the interior as the important and natural site for this work:

> If we cannot yet produce a biologically perfect interior by technological means, our decision must simply be against making an interior fully dependent on intricate technology. We must still design living space, and a current environment for the race, so that the neurological salubrious agents of nature outside are freely admitted and kept active to as great an extent as possible. (Neutra 1954: 195)

In 1954 Neutra outlined these theories in *Survival through Design,* a series of forty-seven essays conveying his observations on the relationships between human psychology, physiology, and the built environment.[2] Hines relates that although the essays were "rich in their multilayered density," they also "tended toward a fragmented, episodic, and elliptical obliqueness." Nonetheless "most critics of the early 1950s received it as a most significant contribution by an architect concerned with the larger environment as well as with its myriad microcosmic components," and *The Nation* predicted that "every architect and planner will read this book" (Hines 1982: 221).

Although Neutra's interest in creating environments that enhanced physical and emotional well-being takes the forefront in his postwar work, that concern, while not outwardly acknowledged, is still recognizable in the earlier work. The integration of nature near and natural light, the emphasis on creating ventilation and maintaining comfortable interior climatic conditions, and the use of easy-to-clean materials as well as the open character of the space of the 1920s and '30s houses all work toward this end. Hines and other authors speculate that Neutra was always interested in this issue because his life was fraught with disease and discomfort. Neutra's grandparents died of typhoid in the 1850s. His mother died of breast cancer in 1905 and his father died of the flu in 1920. His sister went blind and died of a brain tumor at age twenty-seven. Neutra's eldest son, Frank, was born intellectually challenged, and he spent his lifetime considering how a proper healthy environment might improve his son's condition.[3] Neutra himself suffered from tuberculosis and malaria during and after the First World War, and he struggled with his mental health throughout his life, receiving therapy at various times. Many of his letters, writings, and diaries talk about his history of illness and the grinding depressions that plagued him throughout his life. In a 1922 letter to his mother-in-law Lilly Niedermann, he expressed his lifelong concern about his own health in general: "I assure you that I shall try to do everything possible to remain healthy for Dione's sake. I know that health is not ultimate happiness but is surely is a foundation for it" (D. Neutra 1986: 63). One can easily conclude Neutra's commitment and interest in developing health-enhancing spaces were inspired in part by his personal experience. This was certainly the case in the design of his own home and office. Debilitated by two heart attacks in the late '40s and early '50s, Neutra was often forced into bed rest by his doctors. During these periods, he ran his office from his bed through an elaborate multi-purpose command station he designed. A drafting board and easel folded down over his bed while lighting, radio, intercom system, and telephone were built into the bed frame itself to create a space that allowed him, in his own words, to "use every minute from morning to late night" even in his incapacitated state (Hines 1982: 251). Hines reports that many clients described their strange meetings with the architect at this bedstead in which he wore a tie over his pajamas. The many psychological and physical problems that impacted him and his family overlapped with the development of his architectural career and no doubt helped bring together his interest in creating innovative health-enhancing spaces.

But health, hygiene, and the development of life-enhancing space were not solely Neutra's concern, but a less-acknowledged and prominent issue considered by many early European modernists and central to the ethos that shaped Neutra as a designer. Adolf Loos, Neutra's mentor, for example, was at the center of this discussion. In his most famous polemic "Ornament and Crime" of 1908, embraced by the early Modern movement in Europe, Loos outlined an argument against decoration on the basis that it had a pejorative effect on society and was linked with its declining health. He posited: "Not only is ornament produced by criminals but also a crime is committed through the fact that ornament inflicts injury on people's health, on the national budget and hence on cultural evolution" (Conrads 1986: 21). The clean, undecorated, geometrically reduced forms of modernism were his prescription for regenerating society and healing the ill effects of the Victorian period's degenerative visual landscape. For Loos, modern architecture was not merely a stylistic choice but a moral imperative necessary for the improvement of mankind. Following Loos, the influential architect Le Corbusier was also a promoter of a life-enhancing architecture. His use of large expanses of glass to let in light, preference for laboratory-like bathrooms and kitchens with industrialized plumbing and fixtures, use of tubular metal furniture, and inclusion of flat roofs to provide a location for exercise and outdoor activities away from the pollutions of the street were not just formal elements but necessary life-improving amenities. Germany, Italy, and France had initiated state-sponsored sports programs and institutionalized ongoing exercise regimes during the 1920s and '30s that paralleled these developments in early modern architecture. As Leet relates:

> If health and housing reforms represented the socially responsible side of modernity, then sports, dance, and gymnastics represented the spirit of modernity through the ideals of speed, prowess, and the spiritual and physical regeneration of the body. (Leet 2004: 35)

The inclusion of space to enjoy exercise and outdoor activities was an integral feature of early architectural modernism. The links between health, light, and the access to the outdoors were equally stressed as well. Expressionist modern architect Paul Scheerbart, a contemporary and colleague of Neutra's employer in Berlin, Eric Mendelsohn, wrote specifically about the therapeutic nature of glass as a transmitter of natural light:

> If we wish to raise our culture to a higher level, we are forced for better or worse to transform our architecture ... this can be done only through the introduction of glass architecture that lets the sunlight and the light of the moon into our rooms. (Conrads 1964: 32)

In addition to light, the preponderant use of white surfaces in early modern architecture was also linked with efforts to create more life-enhancing, socially transforming, and healthy architecture. In his study on this subject, *White Walls, Designer Dresses: The Fashioning of Modern Architecture*, architectural critic Mark Wigley points out Le Corbusier's particular concern with the hygienic qualities of white surfaces. He says Le Corbusier saw the house as "a habitable surface ... that caters to all the body's needs and thereby frees the mind" (Wigley 1995: 116) and stated that "to walk over a clean surface, to look at an orderly scene" is to "live decently" (Knight 1967: 107). In architecture of the early modern movement, therefore, hygiene, cleanliness, and whiteness were associated with health and social improvement and incorporated into design for that purpose. Richard Neutra would have been familiar with these concepts from his work with Loos in the teens and Mendelsohn in the 1920s as well as through his visits and exchange with prominent European architects and his stay at the Bauhaus in the '30s. As Leet points out in his discussion of Neutra's Miller House: "Hygiene served primarily as an agent of social reform and a bond that linked architecture with health and fitness … Hygiene became an integral aesthetic and ethical component of interwar architecture" (Leet 2004: 34). Although architects such as Marcel Breuer, Walter Gropius, and Mies van der Rohe may have brought the formal vocabulary of International Style Modernism to American shores, Neutra, perhaps more than any other émigré, developed its message of social responsibility, reform, and health in the United States and continued to explore this area far more fully than any of his European colleagues.

Perhaps Neutra's emphasis on this topic also developed in part because of his location in California. In general, the West Coast of the United Sates has provided a much more fertile ground for the message of better health through design. Its moderate climate was perfect for interior designs integrating indoor and outdoor activities, and its fair weather created the ideal setting for promoting healthy outdoor activities through the inclusion of outdoor rooms such as patios, roof decks, and sleeping porches. Even more importantly, California's frontier mentality always has seemed to attract progressive-minded people interested in new theories, new ways of life, and avant-garde thinking. Neutra commented in *Life and Shape*: "In California, especially southern California, I found what I had hoped for, a people who were more 'mentally footloose' than those elsewhere, and who did not mind deviating opinions as long as they were not political. All this seemed to be a good climate for trying something independent of hidebound habituation, European or even American, and also for getting acquainted with human minds and patterns of behavior" (Neutra 1962: 207). The Lovells and Grace Miller, transplants from the East who were interested in developing healthy lifestyles, both chose Neutra as their designer in the late 1920s and early '30s. Neutra shared his belief in therapeutic design with these clients, and his work for them forms the basis of his enhanced environmental/behavioral focus in the '40s and '50s.

The therapeutic interior

A native New Yorker, a practicing naturopath, and anti-drug physician, Philip Lovell advocated natural methods of healing and preventive health care.

He promoted exercise, massage, heat and water cures, open air sleeping, regular nude sunbathing, and a fresh food vegetarian diet in this effort. He also wrote a regular column for the *Los Angeles Times* called "Care of the Body" that disseminated his views. Neutra noted: "Dr. Lovell wanted to be a patron of forward-looking experiment. He would be the man who could see health and future in a strange wide-open filigree steel frame, set deftly and precisely by cranes and booms into this inclined piece of ragged nature" (Neutra 1962: 221). In the Lovell House, Neutra attempted to integrate Lovell's theories on health and fitness into the design of their home. Open air sleeping porches, terraces for nude sunbathing, showers and sitz baths, a kitchen for natural cooking, a swimming pool, an open-air theater, and places for tennis, handball, and basketball were all incorporated. The interiors were constructed of materials in soothing natural colors that were easy to clean and maintain, thereby causing less stress and worry. Large expanses of glass let in natural light all through the space. Throughout the interior, green plants enlivened and softened the space and recycled the carbon dioxide. The garden was designed with exercise equipment in it like sculpture. Lovell wrote in his newspaper column: "We have built ... a home premised on the fundamental health principles and construction ideas which I have presented in my writings ... it is unquestionably the very best combination of the utmost utilitarianism and beauty" (Hines 1982: 89). He encouraged his readers to copy the ideas he used in his house, and together with Neutra he hosted open houses at the site. Over 15,000 people came to visit and the publicity gained through this venture thrust Neutra not only to the forefront of modern design on the West Coast but identified him as a designer who was particularly interested in the interconnection of health and the built environment. In one of his late essays he reflected on his position on this:

> If regular muscular exercise is important to the physical and mental health of our evolving urban dweller, and if the architect's job is to accomplish something more wholesome than merely saving steps, then places for exercise will have to become a commonplace feature. This will include providing living arrangements that afford real privacy, along with nearby options for recreation, exercise and socializing all of which measureable help nervously creative, incessantly involved individual who are feeling pressured and stressed. (Neutra in Marlin 1989: 95)

Neutra described the Lovell House in his autobiography as a kind of medicine which provided "a full dose of environment ... over at least a thirty-year amortization period" (Neutra 1962: 220) and in his practice he began to see himself as a kind of designer/doctor.[4]

His client Grace Lewis Miller also shared Neutra and Lovell's concern for the development of physical and mental well-being. Miller was a student and teacher of the Mensendieck system, an exercise program then being promoted in the United States particularly to women, that encouraged the development of muscle strength, alignment, and proper postures as a way of improving beauty and health. Bess Mensendieck was a Dutch physician who developed the series of more than 200 exercises in 1906 that taught correct body alignment and breathing in everyday actions for the purpose of overcoming the strain placed on the body by poor posture and environmental stresses. Daily exercises were properly performed naked in front of a mirror so that the student could observe the body's positions more accurately. Followers of this method, which is still practiced today, claim increased vitality, strength, and sense of well-being. Current Mensendieck method therapist Karen Perlroth relates that creating a relationship between mind and body is an important component of the practice.

When Grace Miller moved to Palm Springs, California, from St. Louis, Missouri, after her husband died in 1936, it was a resort town and vacation site for movie stars and wealthy businessmen and their families. Miller envisioned it as good location to start a new life and to promote her classes in the Mensendieck method to the "beautiful people" who populated the area. Neutra was familiar with the Mensendieck method from his early modernist training in Europe and shared his knowledge and enthusiasm for it with Miller when they first met in Los Angles in 1936. Leet says that "Neutra's interest in physical culture and his preoccupation with the recuperative effects that he believed architecture had on health and well-being made him ideally suited for the Miller House commission" (Leet 2004: 61). He agreed to build the house in 1937 under the condition it be referred to as the Mensendieck House and designed a small but luxurious 1200-square-foot house on a desert site in Palm Springs for Miller. Following Neutra's basic approach in the '30s, the house was a simple pavilion made of concrete with his signature silver-gray aluminum trim on the exterior. The interior was a simple, open plan that aligned the closed spaces of bedrooms, baths, and kitchen against a large open area that contained the living/teaching area and porch. In plan the house echoes the two major techniques of the Mensendieck method: contraction and extension. The large open living space, which is expanded by the screen porch and the view of the vista beyond, allows the interior to fully extend out, creating both a psychological and physical openness (Figure 2.5). The bath, kitchen, and bedroom have fewer windows and are compressed together and turned inward, creating a sense of center, limit, and closeness. Together the two sections reflect what therapist Karen Perlroth would describe in physiological terms as the "balanced antagonism of flexor and extensor." In all its aspects, the interior shows its "good posture" in its lean vertical lines of its windows and door frames balanced by its solid horizontal built-in features. When the drapes that cover all the windows are drawn back the house reveals its true beauty in its "nakedness" just as the Mensendieck student does when practicing the required exercises. Neutra emphasizes the "good bones" and "posture" of the building by using the lean lines and various industrialized, sleek materials such as stainless steel and glass block of his earlier work, here used purposely to enhance the overall healthy qualities of the house as a physical reflection of the Mensendieck philosophy. The house's interaction with the environment also accentuates its therapeutic aspects. Both the screened porch and the expanses of windows are designed to emphasize the views of the desert terrain and to integrate the interior with the exterior. Photographs of the interior of the house demonstrate the feeling that the interior space projects into the view.

At the same time the sparse furnishings and emphasis on open space in the interior seem to replicate the spatial arrangement of the vertical low growing plants that break up the expansive roll of the desert in a rhythmic pattern. The colors of the desert are replicated in the interior in a subtle palette of rust, brown, and white to create a soothing effect. Mirrors on the inside replicate the expansiveness of the desert and extend the apparent boundaries of an extremely small space, allowing one to feel sheltered and protected yet open and unconfined. Perhaps even more importantly, the house is designed in a way that allows the interaction of the occupant with fresh air and sunshine, regardless of the potentially harsh conditions of the desert and the weather (Figure 2.2). Wide overhangs on the east, south, and west sides temper the direct sunlight and solar gain. Screened ventilation soffits allow fresh air to flow through the space. A covered pool adjacent to the screen porch and large open living room modulate the heat and provide beautiful reflective patterns. In the Miller House the body is able to assume its natural place in nature. Neutra himself explained the therapeutic impact of the design and its "nature near" concept for enhancing well-being:

The Mensendieck House in Palm Springs represents modern man's nearness to nature, his new approach to biologically correct modes of living, with bodies which are beautiful, because they move and act as nature has designed them to move and act because they are not shut off from the healthful rays and wholesome air. (Leet 2004: 60)

Like the Lovell House, the Miller House was highly publicized, this time using the stunning photography of the now legendary photographer Julius Shulman, who was able to capture the exquisite character of the space and its integration with its environment.[5] Both the Lovell and Miller Houses were not only a springboard to Neutra's advancing career and reputation but catapulted him to the forefront of the emerging field of environmental design and its concern for creating healthy life-enhancing spaces. By the 1940s and '50s Neutra was continuously employed by a long list of clients whose primary concern was to "go modern" for the sake of life enhancement and improved well-being. Teachers, artists, advocates of "new-age" religions, and philosophers, as well as forward-thinking businessmen, came to Neutra for his particular brand of modern house. The consistently positive reports from the owners and occupants of the houses attest that they believed Neutra's strategies worked. Bertha Mosk, whose house Neutra designed in 1933, stated that her home enhanced the "feeling that now we have freedom to breathe and grow. The house is alive and so we too feel vital" (D. Neutra 1986: 229). Ruth Beebe Hill wrote on Neutra's work in her essay, "Fitting Life with a Shell," that "Richard Neutra is able to design a structure which makes the people who live it in now or forever, 'feel good.'" (Ruth Beebe Hill, "Fitting Life with a Shell"; quoted in Lavin, 68). In the 1950s Neutra described the elation the new owner of the Nesbitt House experienced when she discovered how her full-paned glass doors could open totally to the outside, thus transforming her outlook:

> It was like magic to her, a discovery of a new spring of life, like someone discovering, imagine, that he can spread winds and fly! There was wild dancing on the lawn: I received a kiss, several kisses and we all got drunk. (Letter from RJN to Orline Moore, April 25, 1950, Neutra Archive)

In his desire to create nurturing spaces that incorporate the tenets of his theories of bio-realism, Neutra perhaps more than his contemporaries responded vigorously to the criticism in the postwar period that modern architecture was cold, sterile, and difficult to inhabit. As a result, the hard, white, metal, machine-like surfaces of his 1930s houses dissolved into a new palette of texture and warmth. California redwood replaced the concrete and steel structural members of his earlier buildings. Brick and stone were used on floors both inside and outside, textile wall covering and knobby, earthy fabrics were employed for the interior surfaces. The Nesbitt House of 1942 provides one of the first examples of this new turn that was later to be developed in his Case Study house for *Arts and Architecture* magazine for Stuart Bailey (1947), the Hinds House (1951), Moore House (1952), Perkins House (1955), and Nash House (1957) (Figure 2.6). In all these interiors Neutra's concepts of "nature near," his use of life-enhancing technology, his clean, simplified formal vocabulary, his concern for the life-enhancing impact of all aspects of the designs are translated into a new palette of warm color, wood, stone, brick, and other natural materials. In the Nesbitt House, designed for NBC producer John Nesbitt, Neutra replaced the formulaic standard flat roof of the International Style with a gently pitched shed roof that folded down over that rear glass wall to create a protective overhang. Floors and fireplaces were brick, and board and batten redwood covered the exterior, while other wood walls and accents were used in the interior. A lily pool outside the front entrance extended beneath the glass into the interior hallway and gently undulating brick wall outlined the patio, creating one of Neutra's hallmark exterior/interior spaces.

In the interior, Neutra continued his tradition of horizontal lines, built-in furniture, flexibility of spaces, and large expanses of glass that integrate the interior with the exterior. But as Sylvia Lavin and others point out, the overall effect is much more sensuous, tactile and bodily. Hard and soft materials are used adjacently to create visual and tactile contrast. Aluminum, terrazzo, and vinyl materials, which deflect heat, cover surfaces the body is most likely to touch. These are contrasted with the hard, cool surfaces of cabinetry and floors. The rough fabric of the drapes purposely contrasts with the cool planes of glass and the flattened photograph-like view of the exterior beyond. Mitered butt-glazed glass corners provide ambiguity and simultaneous feelings of containment and openness. Lavin says that the interiors are "moody" and "shift from habit forming neutrality to a surprising confrontation" (Lavin 2004: 110). The house won a first-place award from AIA and comments from the jury concur with Lavin's observations: "Urban sophistication and cultural refinement have been expressed in terms of almost rustic simplicity—a juxtaposition of contrasting moods that is, in part, the key to the tantalizing delightfulness of the house" (Hines 1982: 199). Once again the occupants verified the positive impact this approach to design had on their lives. Stuart Bailey, owner of Case Study House #20, commented that his home "does not just sit here passively. I feel that it acts on me in a most beneficial manner. It draws me to it" (Hines: 211). Constance Perkins wrote that by commissioning a Neutra house she believed she had found the means "for making life so happy" (Letter from Constance Perkins to R. Neutra, May 31, 1956). Josephine Ain, wife of Robert Chuey, wrote to Neutra about their home:

> This house has the quality of an absolute presence. You are an alchemist who has transmuted earth, house, and sky into a single enchantment … This house seems to have a spiritual existence … It remembers that being is a miracle. I can only hope that I can in some measure grow up to the wholes and balance embodied here. (Hines: 261)

The Chueys also claimed their house plan increased their productivity and creativity because it made them happy and reduced distractions and stresses:

> We are more and more inspired and feel that after we have savored the house in its own soul we will ourselves prove more productive both as to

volume and quality of our work. (Letter from Josephine and Robert Chuey to R. Neutra, July 8, 1955 Neutra Archive)

This energizing, elevating, and life-enhancing impact on the occupants of Neutra's interiors is well-documented. Sylvia Lavin advances the interesting theory that the interiors of Neutra's postwar houses work much the same way as the now infamous contemporary "orgone boxes" popularized by the psychoanalyst Wilhelm Reich. Reich speculated that the energies of the universe—from radioactive particles to the biochemical reaction or orgasm—had commonality, and the key to well-being was collecting and channeling and directing this energy where needed. He called this universal category of energy "orgone." Starting in 1940 he designed and constructed large boxes made from a combination of cotton, glass, wood, rock, polyethylene, steel wool, and galvanized sheet metal. These materials supposedly contained orgone energy, and the boxes, therefore, collected and focused that energy in one place. Clients would sit in the boxes to be bombarded by the collected energy in the box, which would supposedly cure a variety of ills from cancer to impotence and depression. Both the environment and the body could be improved by this treatment. Lavin proposes that varied and contrasting natural materials used in the interiors of Neutra's late work act like Reich's orgone boxes. Their walls, ceilings, and floors were reliefs built of such materials as wood, metal stone, paint, cork, and fabric that, she says, created a particular kind of visual, aesthetic, and psychic energy that made its occupants feel good. She posits: 'His later houses did not just provide a place to eat macrobiotically and do calisthenics but claimed to enhance what Neutra called "psycho-physiological wholeness" (Lavin 2004: 86). She further speculates that the transcendental state of well-being claimed by the orgone box therapy is replicated in the Neutra interior: "One improved oneself by sitting alone in an orgone box or living in a Neutra House just as previous generations had improved themselves through individual communion with God" (Lavin 2004).

As Lavin proposes, it is perhaps not coincidental that this period of Neutra's career overlaps with the rise in popularity of psychoanalysis and a general interest in psychologies of all kinds in the postwar United States. Within this trend, Neutra's emphasis on the individual in his or her environment as a generator of form seems particularly appropriate. Although Neutra's career developed during a period of modernism notable for its universalist solutions and advocacy of standardization, he always demonstrated a marked interest in the individualized and the particular. "The 'individual' himself is truly not divisible," he wrote, "and the very word stems from this insight ... he has not sharp barriers around him, but rather permeable membranes. He keeps absorbing through them. He has no existence in a vacuum or apart from an outer world" (Neutra 1962: 12). Neutra believed in knowing the client on a personal level, and, as his wife Dione reported, extending himself to go so far as to even "fall in love with them" to design their home (Hines, 255). Knowing his clients and being empathetic with them were an important part of his process. In *Life and Shape* he wrote: "Without empathy, that subconscious in-feeling, no architect-planner (who is an artist, too) can produce anything but a stillborn environment for his clients, however, logically and carefully worked out and consistently constructed" (Neutra 1962: 11). Clients were required to complete an extensive survey designed by Neutra in which he asked them to express both their functional and emotional needs as well as their expectations for their living spaces before he began their design. They often likened the process to psychoanalysis and frequently took weeks to complete the process. He wrote: "An architect producing by proper means of rapport with the client's aspirations and expressed or half-expressed need is actually acting very closely to the pattern of procedure of a psychiatrist ... Architecture should operate like psychotherapy by assisting clients to satisfy unconscious psychical desires" (Neutra 1954). Neutra acted like a doctor: first learning all he could know about his patient and then making a diagnosis about how to improve their health through the design of their space. He understood the power of his bedside manner. "A doctor gains almost magical powers if we trust him fully," he wrote in *Life and Shape* (Neutra 1962: 91).

In this respect Neutra evidences the influence of the work of the psychologist Wilhelm Wundt, author of *Principles of Physiological Psychology* (1873). When asked in the 1960s what books design students should be reading he recommended only Wundt's book (Isenstadt 2000: 103). Wundt had established one of the first psychology labs in the world in Leipzig in 1879. He believed that the emerging field of psychology needed to be rooted in empirical study. Like Wundt, Neutra thought that scientific observation and the study of the physiological and psychological impact of the components of interior design on its users was essential to the creation of a life-enhancing environment. Neutra's client interview was part of this necessary examination and study of human needs that he always attempted to integrate into his designs. Neutra's study of theories of psychology and behavior, from his earlier and personal interaction with the theories of Sigmund Freud to the study of Wilhelm Wundt, as well as the more questionable ideas of Wilhelm Reich's "orgone" energy, are all used by him in his pursuit of creating healthy, therapeutic interiors in the 1950s and '60s. This idea that the development of one's personality and fulfillment of physical and mental needs are interrelated with the design of one's interior environment forms the basis of Neutra's approach to the design for the rest of his career.

Neutra's legacy

Neutra's designs were highly publicized and well-distributed for modern consumption in such popular mainstream shelter magazines such as *Better Homes and Gardens* and *Ladies Home Journal*. Architectural and design magazines, including *Architectural Forum* and *Interiors*, also frequently published his work. Between 1949 and 1956 *Interiors* magazine featured Neutra's work at least five times, establishing it as exemplary in the field. In 1947, his design for Case Study House #20, the Bailey House, was published as part of the now famous program sponsored by *Arts and Architecture* magazine. Also, in 1947, *Time* magazine included a feature story on him, which was followed up in 1949 by a cover story that propelled him to the forefront in American design. In addition, his own writings were published in numerous periodicals. The publication of his books, *The Architecture of Social Concern* (1948) and *Survival by Design* (1954), made his particular philosophies and concerns for socially responsible and life-enhancing designs well-known. In the 1960s, Neutra set up a non-profit organization to promote communication between design, planning, and scientific professions to support his interest (Hines 1982: 131). Also during this decade Kevin Lynch, head of the urban design program at MIT, asked him to serve as a consultant to help the university develop an environmental psychology program. Neutra's son Raymond pursued a career in environmental medicine and eventually became the Chief of the Division of Environmental and Occupational Disease Control of the California Department of Public Health. His oldest son Dion became an architect and continued Neutra's work in his design practice after he died.

Neutra's rise to prominence parallels not only the development of the modern style in the United States, but the emergence of both environmental and interior design as academic and professional disciplines. His focus on understanding the human psyche and its behavior and needs was particularly appropriate for these developing fields, which focuses on the intimate actions and reactions of bodies with a designed space.

Neutra's theory of bio-realism and his concern for both psychological and behavioral issues, while admired and absorbed by interior design, became less admired by architects by the late 1960s, when many turned away from behaviorist approaches and embraced the theoretical premises of postmodernism and deconstruction. In his later career and until his death in 1970, Neutra's reputation as a modern architect was overshadowed and perhaps even diminished by his psycho-physiological approach to design as this poetic parody of him published in the August 1956 Journal of the AIA entitled "Homesick" clearly illustrates:

"This House is a mess and it's driving me mad"
Home dwellers have fizzed through the ages.
"The planning's disastrous, the outlook is bad!
It's giving me rabies-like rages!
And that damned interior design not only vexes
It's bringing on big red hives, and black complexes!"
Yes, that's how it's been, Richard Neutra explains
In a tone that's both cheery and mordant.
Poor wretches have suffered unclassified pains
When their backgrounds were vilely discordant.
But now we have grown wise, we can psychiatrize,
By grace of science, all such miseries we can Neutra-lize.
So now let's build houses to drive people normal
And make the wild client go mild.
The textures, shapes, hues shall be gently reformal,
Fierce couples shall be reconciled.   ·
A bratty tot can be a darling (or quite near it)
When the architect's got therapeutic spirit.
Devising sound dwellings might do in the past
But a new era dictates new roles.
Today's Master Builder's portentously cast,
For he must design clients' souls.
He must build in that psychic neutra-ment for life protection.
Homes are health centers, house of correction.
(But, come now A.I.A., what next?
The A.M.A. looks rather vexed!)

Nonetheless Richard Neutra created a particular brand of modern interior that focused more than any other designer of his time on the health and welfare of the individual, leaving behind a legacy of compelling, livable, and enjoyable modern interiors. As Norman Cousins stated in his forward to William Marlins collection of Neutra's essays, Richard Neutra's "cascading enthusiasm for life" was "an oxygenating force with a deep understanding of man's exquisitely sensitive spiritual tissue, he saw architecture as a means of nurturing and exalting that sensitivity. By pointing up the therapeutic utility of harmonious surroundings, whether at the level of the individual dwelling or the urban streetscape, he was serving a more complete sense of practical human function" (Marlin 1989: viii). Neutra's focus on bettering the human condition through their environment and his indefatigable belief in his own responsibility to improve peoples' lives allowed him to create a most powerful and effective kind of modern interior.

3

The Eames House and
a New Language of Vision

Most people have experienced the work of Ray and Charles Eames, although they might not know it. Their ubiquitous molded plywood and fiberglass chairs that were designed and developed in the early 1950s still dot our interior landscapes, schools, and offices, denoting a modern aesthetic, forward-looking attitude and a contemporary kind of space. Their more luxurious rosewood lounge chair and ottoman was strategically placed on the set of the long-running American television show *Frasier* as an icon that designated a sophisticated kind of masculinity and allowed an inestimable-sized audience to enjoy the design every time they tuned in. In 1962, the *Los Angeles* magazine speculated that "more than two million people, conservatively, could sit simultaneously on the various Eames chairs sold thus far" (*Los Angeles* magazine 1962: 24). The mind staggers to think what that number would be now. During their lifetime the Eameses, as a couple, were probably the most successful and respected of American modern designers. Their design office set up in 1941 in their apartment building designed by Richard Neutra in Westwood, California—later relocated to their well-known location in Venice, both near Los Angeles—was a center for some of the most creative design thinking of its time. Although primarily noted for their innovations in product and furniture design and later visual communications, Ray and Charles Eames's contribution to interior design was also significant, particularly their home completed in 1949, which many consider one of the most influential interiors of the postwar period.

But the design of the Eames house is not without its criticisms. Analysis of the interior in particular over the years has proved especially problematic to some scholars because of its seemingly dichotomous nature, heavily documented in photographs, which show the combination of a straightforward modernist structure with what has been often described as "Victorian clutter"

(McCoy 1973: 67) and an excess of objects in its interior design (Figure 3.1). The particular condition was unavoidably noticeable to anyone who visited the house, described as being filled with "lovingly positioned collections of shells, baskets, blankets, mats, candles, pillows, pots, plants, sculpture, chairs" (Carpenter 1979: 13). Although this "clutter of the objects" was referred

FIGURE 3.1 *Interior of the Eames House, Alcove Sitting Area, c. 1950s. (Courtesy of the Eames Office, © 2018 Eames Office, LLC, eamesoffice.com. Photo: Timothy Street Porter, 1994).*

to by the Eameses as "functioning decoration" and defended in terms of function, materials, and structure, most critics have found the resulting decorative nature of the interior unsettling and often categorize it as reflective of a feminized, decorative, and non-Modern impulse usually ascribed to Ray Eames. This interesting character of the Eames design and the questions it raises will be more fully considered here. Why was this insistent layering of numerous and diverse kinds of objects so important? What purpose did it truly serve, since knowing the attention to detail exhibited by the couple, it could certainly not be accidental nor simply personally indulgent? What was their concept and purpose of doing this? In considering these questions, one can speculate that the Eames house does not present a dichotomous interior and exterior springing from different concerns, but reflects a holistic design inspired and driven by the Eameses' theoretical investigation into the nature of vision, particularly theories about a new "language of vision" as being propagated by the abstract expressionist painter, Hans Hofmann, Ray Eames's New York mentor and teacher, and the artist/designer György Kepes, the couples' friend and colleague. Inspired by and resonating with these sources, the couple created a uniquely modern, yet uniquely Eames interpretation of what contemporary living should be.

The architect and the artist

Charles Eames was the son of a Pinkerton guard, who inherited both his father's camera and interest in photography, which expressed itself in the countless documentation photos taken over the years for himself and for the Eames Office. He was not schooled in photography, however. Eames's formal education was in architecture at Washington University in St. Louis, a fairly conservative school still teaching in the Beaux-Arts tradition during the time Charles attended. His interest in creating modern designs and inability to conform to the school's values caused him to be considered a "progressive thinker" and he was asked to leave in 1928 for "showing too much enthusiasm for the work of Frank Lloyd Wright" (Kirkham 1995: 12). This experience never deterred him from a career in architecture, however, and he began working for a major firm in St. Louis, Trueblood and Graf where he resumed his training. He soon after opened his own office in 1930 and continued to be interested in modern developments while participating in St. Louis's contemporary art and intellectual scene. He traveled to Europe in 1929 on his honeymoon with his first wife Catherine Woermann and studied European modernism first-hand. He returned to the United States to practice architecture working in what has been described as a modern and eclectic kind of Arts and Crafts mode but struggled to be successful. In 1933, he left behind his wife and new daughter to do an eight-month solo road trip to Mexico. Biographer Pat Kirkham explains: "He himself found it difficult to scrape a living, but it was the concomitant psychological depression that finally made him leave the city and reassess his life" (Kirkham 1995: 16). After this re-centering trip which reports say consisted of wandering, exploring, meeting local people, drawing as well as drinking and spending a night or two in jail, he returned to St. Louis to set up a new practice with Robert Walsh in 1934. Eames and Walsh produced enough successful work to come to the attention of Eliel Saarinen who offered Charles a fellowship at Cranbrook Academy of Art in 1938. Although Eames reportedly accepted the position so that he could withdraw from his work life and "reflect and read" he soon launched fully into the projects going on there. Impressed by his work, Saarinen soon appointed him as Instructor of Design in what evolved to be the Department of Industrial Design (or as he called it Experimental Design). He also worked with both Eliel and Eero Saarinen in their design practice. The Cranbrook experience was a turning point for Charles Eames, giving him both access to an incredible group of designers like Eero Saarinen, who continuing his modernist training, and the fortuitous introduction to his soon-to-be partner and wife, Ray Kaiser.

Ray Kaiser arrived at Cranbrook in 1940 and met Charles Eames while helping him prepare drawings for the *Organic Furniture* competition at the Museum of Modern Art (MoMA). By the end of the experience, as their grandson Eames Demetrios reports, "They were hooked on each other" (Demetrios 2002: 96). In 1941 Charles finalized his divorce and he and Ray married and moved to California where they started their lifelong collaboration. Born and raised in California, Ray Kaiser and her mother had moved to New York in 1931 to be closer to her brother who attended West Point. Ray was trained as a painter and from 1933 to 1939 she lived in or around New York City and was a student of the abstract expressionist painter Hans Hofmann at his schools both in New York and in Provincetown. Kaiser was a popular student at the schools affectionately known as "Buddha" and Hofmann trained her in the tenets of abstract art. She was a founding member of the American Abstract Association and exhibited work in its first show at the Manhattan Municipal Art Galleries in the mid-1930s. Her artwork was a playful kind of organic abstraction, with curving shapes and bright colors and her understanding of color, aesthetics, and form developed during these years seemed to be the perfect complement to Charles's knowledge of structure, architecture, and photography when they came together as a design team at Cranbrook.

Charles Eames was pushed to the forefront of the American design scene when in partnership with Eero Saarinen he won first prize for their molded chair experiments in two categories of the *Organic Designs in Home*

Furnishings competition sponsored by MoMA in 1940. These designs became the prototypes and foundation for the Eameses' ongoing experiments in furniture design during the 1940s. After moving to Los Angeles, Charles and Ray continued experimenting with molded plywood forms in the makeshift workshop they set up first in their apartment and later in the Eames Office in Venice. The story of the machine they invented to mold plywood, how it took up most of the space in their living quarters and made the noise "Kazam" that would later be its name is notorious. In 1946 Eames was given a one-man show at the MoMA and later was part of their *International Competition for Low Cost Housing* in 1948. These shows at the museum were important in bringing Eames's work into the public spotlight, as well as to the attention of George Nelson who was the design director at the Herman Miller Furniture Company at the time. Herman Miller began mass-producing and distributing the Eameses' products in 1946. Their work for Herman Miller propelled Charles into international recognition and jumped started both their careers in which they explored modern design in furniture, industrial products, interiors, architecture, exhibition design, and film for over thirty years.[1]

The Eames house

In a campaign to promote modern design within the housing boom of the postwar period, John Entenza, editor of *Arts and Architecture* magazine, initiated the Case Study House program which sponsored the design, construction, public exhibition, and test in use of modern houses in the southern California area from 1945 to 1966. The Case Study House program provided trained architects the opportunity to present their ideas about modern architecture by finding both clients and financing for them. By its close in 1966, twenty-eight houses had been designed, built, and opened to the public. Over 368,000 people toured these houses and the program was lauded as "one of the most distinguished and influential architectural programs ever inaugurated" (McCoy 1977: 10). The Eameses had been associated with *Arts and Architecture* since the early 1940s, when Charles worked as an editorial associate and Ray was part of its advisory board and designed magazine covers for the publication. Charles had also been a judge for the *Design for Post War Living* competition that Entenza had organized in 1943 and agreed with Entenza about the need to not only create new housing ideas but to test by building them. Eames full heartedly entered the Case Study House project and was involved in the design of two houses, his own (Number 8) in collaboration with this wife, and the house for John Entenza (Number 9) in collaboration with Eero Saarinen. Both houses share a site in Pacific Palisades but in form and concept are very different. Although they use a similar formula of materials, the Entenza house is more a modern translation of a grand manor house with large spaces for entertaining, sweeping views, and a multi-car garage, while the Eames house could be seen an interpretation of a cozy bungalow and workshop in its scale and purpose. In December 1945, the first design for the Eames house was published in *Arts and Architecture* as part of its promulgation of the Case Study House program. This early idea for the house is generally attributed to "the Eames office, working with Eero Saarinen" (Kirkham 1995: 106) although Ray Eames later stated that the entire Eames Office had participated in it, giving her also a place in its initial creation. The house was completely re-designed by both the Eameses in 1947 and built in 1949.

The final design of the house is a simple rectilinear plan constructed from prefabricated parts that consists of two separate pavilions—one for living and one for working (Figure 3.2). The arrangement of the parts, colors, and materials in the house's engineered framework creates a grid-like structure that has been often visually associated by some with the work of the modern abstract artist, Piet Mondrian. The building was specifically sited along a row of ten eucalyptus trees that existed on the far end of an open meadow. The

FIGURE 3.2 *Exterior of the Eames House, c. 1950s. (© J. Paul Getty Trust. Getty Research Institute, Los Angeles, 2004.R.10. Photo: Julius Shulman).*

couple took great pains to build their house behind the trees by excavating the hill adjacent to them and building a retaining wall, 8 feet high and 175 feet long, to realize their scheme. The interior structure, whose exposed metal framework is "skeletal as in an airplane fuselage," creates a light, airy, and open effect both vertically and horizontally (C. Eames 1950: 94). An overhanging sleeping gallery with an alcove below is the only enclosed space and functions to divide the living and dining areas. Sliding glass doors and windows allow for a large amount of light, transparency of space, and a view of the outdoors. The light steel frame of the interior is painted dark gray and left exposed. Large expanses of walls are painted neutral colors or left as natural wood while accents of bright color and arrangements of simple modern furniture embellish the space.

By the 1950s the house accumulated a number of objects whose arrangement became an important, if not essential, part of the completed interior design. The placement of these objects was reported to be extremely planned. Pat Kirkham, the Eameses' biographer, noted that "Ray was constantly shifting objects until that looked just right" (Kirkham 1995: 188). Audrey Wilder, wife of the director and Eames client Billy Wilder and a frequent visitor to the house, remembers "how neat and precise everything was" and reported that before an evening of entertaining Ray would make sure that the candles had burned down to a certain height and that every pillow and plant was positioned (Kirkham 1995). The Eameses' own many documentations of their home that include these numerous objects confirm their importance to them as part of the design (Figures 3.1, 3.3). When questioned about these objects in their house, the Eameses always discussed them "within the framework of the functionalism that dominated the discourse of design" (C. Eames 1950: 145). However, in their display the visual effects of the objects rather than their instructive qualities were always emphasized. As Kirkham observed of the Eameses' use of their collection of Hopi kachina dolls: "Yet, although Charles and Ray insisted that these remarkable objects—the spirit essences of things and customs in the real world—could be understood only in the context of Hopi history and culture, the example we were discussing was mainly used for decorative effect on the sofa" (C. Eames 1950).

The importance of the visual quality of these objects and the somewhat obsessive behavior Ray Eames demonstrated in their arrangement points to both Eameses' concern with the construction of the visual field as the primary generator of the design of their house. When closely studied, photographs of the interiors and the objects themselves confirm neither "Victorian clutter" nor a typical well-decorated household, but a precisely planned and constructed formal vision. The Eames film, House: After 5 Years of Living, which is made up of hundreds of single images of the residence, documents this formal and visual emphasis. The Eameses' need to create this film only confirms

FIGURE 3.3 *Interior of the Eames House, c. 1950s (© J. Paul Getty Trust. Getty Research Institute, Los Angeles, 2004.R.10. Photo: Julius Shulman).*

the couple's interest in the visual as the primary concern of its design. The documentation of the actual use of this building throughout the years also reinforces the primacy of its visual aspects to the Eames. After the house was built, its aesthetics and visual qualities always took precedence over modernist functionalism. Don Albinson and Richard Donges, Eames employees who took care of the property, reported that the house was often a maintenance nightmare. The sea air, weathering, and dampness wreaked havoc on the exterior that had to be cleaned monthly to remove sea salt and eucalyptus oil. The roof leaked, and there was inadequate drainage. Neuhart reported that the heating system was notoriously inadequate and when asked once what the heating source for the house was, Charles Eames pointed to the sweater he was wearing. Donges noted that during the time that he was in charge of repairs, he was at the Eameses' home two and three times a week. Changes in the house were never implemented to overcome these problems; instead, the visual integrity and formal impact of the house were vigilantly maintained (J. and M. Neuhart 1994: 53).

A new language of vision

The fact that the visual construction of the house was the primary focus of this design is not surprising, considering the background and training of the Eameses and their contemporary context in postwar America. Both Ray and Charles Eames were visual artists as well as designers. She trained with Hans Hofmann in the postwar school of modern abstraction, while he was a self-trained yet dedicated photographer and filmmaker. Their diverse work throughout their career is linked by their interest in the act of seeing and in creating controlled arranged views to be seen. As well, all the Eameses' work consistently demonstrates their belief that seeing is a creative process that expands and educates the intellectual field of the viewer. As Charles remarked in his notes for the Frank Nelson Doubleday Lecture he gave at the Smithsonian in 1977: "Each has the need to come to grips with a cogent and highly informative 'language of vision.' Words well used can tell everything, given time, but current, highly structured data often cries out to be modeled by visual images that can change along a time axis" (C. Eames 1977: Eames Archive, Box 217, Folder 14, 5).

For Ray Eames, this primacy for the visual field came from her training as an artist and particularly from Hofmann who introduced her to the language of abstract formalism. Hans Hofmann was one of the few members of the New York School who had participated directly in the early Modern movement in Europe. As a young painter he studied in Paris and became familiar with the work of many prominent artists during the period, but his ideas were shaped particularly by the pictorial deconstructions of Cubism as well as by the color explorations of the Fauves, which he developed into a systematic pedagogy for teaching. Art historian Robert Hobbs explains in his discussion of Hofmann's influence on Ray Eames's fellow student and friend Lee Krasner:

Hofmann's lectures emphasized three essential factors: nature, the artist's temperament, and the limits of the medium. Each factor had its own laws, and no one had priority over the other. Hofmann counseled his students ... that colors interacted in a way that could be understood abstractly in terms of the "push-pull" between hues. Instead of overlapping forms to suggest depth, he preferred students to create tensions between planes so that the inherent two-dimensionality of the canvas would be maintained. (Hobbs 1993: 23)

In his work, planes and colors that moved forward in space counteracted the receding movement of other elements. Against a structural background that was laid onto the canvas, which he referred to as "first lines," layering of forms, transparencies, contrasts in hue, value, and warmth of color were manipulated to set up the juxtapositions of oppositional elements that created the "push/pull" effect. Paul Ellsworth in a 1949 article on Hofmann further explains: "To create the phenomenon of 'push and pull' on a flat surface one has to understand that by nature the picture plane automatically reacts in the opposite direction to the stimulus received; this action continues as long as it receives stimulus in the creative process" (Goldstein and McCoy 1990: 117).

Hofmann made the analogy that the process of push/pull was like nudging a gas-filled balloon from one side and then the other. He also posited that the push/pull phenomenon was not only a visual and physical experience but a spiritual one. For Hofmann, the contrapuntal forces at work on the canvas reflected both the positive and negative experiences in life. An understanding of push/pull in observing the world and translating it on the canvas thus facilitated a better understanding of those basic forces. His theory of push/pull was the primary focus in his formalized pedagogy of teaching abstract art. A student of Hofmann's learned this concept as a "mode of plastic creation" and a way of seeing and organizing the visual world. Although she was exposed to many artists practicing modern art in the 1930s, Ray Eames identified her experience with Hofmann as a "great part of my life" (Demetrios 2002: 75) and pages of her notes of his lectures that she recorded while taking classes with him in the early 1930s dominate her personal files in the Eames Office archive at the Library of Congress. For Ray Eames, her practice of design was always an extension of her interest in art and reflective of her training with Hofmann. As she stated when asked about moving from painting to design: "I never gave up painting, I just changed my palette" (Demetrios 2002: 75). Her husband also acknowledged Hofmann's great influence on her visual acuity:

She has a very good sense of what gives an idea, or form, or piece of sculpture its character, of how its relationships are formed. She can see

when there is a wrong mix of ideas or materials, where the division
between two ideas isn't clear. If this sounds like a structural or architectural
idea, it is. But it comes to Ray through her painting ... any student of Hans's
has a sense of this kind of structure. (Carpenter 1979: 10)

Ray Eames brought the lessons of her early training with Hofmann into
play in her paintings, her graphic designs for covers of *Arts and Architecture*
magazine, textile designs, numerous drawings and collages created for Eames
Office projects as well as the design of the Eames house. Photographs of
the interior show the plethora of objects noted by critics, but also document
a precisely planned and constructed visual composition (Figure 3.3). The
primary importance of the objects is clearly their visual quality not their
function, sentiment, or educational value. Pillows are carefully stacked with
edges matching to illustrate specific arrangement of materials, colors, and
textures. Rugs and coverings were layered on the floors, walls, and ceilings
to create a push/pull of surface and depth as well as warmth and coolness.
Objects are carefully hung and placed in relationship to built-in elements. This
layering of objects contrasts with the open space and minimalist planes of the
interior forms and also activates them. Paintings are hung from the ceiling,
creating a surprising contradiction when one tries to read the ceiling plane
and the volume of the space, pushing the eye away from deep perspective
into the flat perspective of the picture plane. A tumbleweed or piece of folk
art suspended in a corner interrupts the flat wall planes and adds sense of
movement or gesture. Reflections in the large expanses of windows interact
with the vertical lines of the drapes, the objects in the interior, and the play
of light through the window creating a dynamic interplay. This disruption of
the pictorial space of the room reflects Hofmann's principle of push/pull in
which he notes: "Depth, in a pictorial, plastic sense, is not created by the
arrangement of objects one after another toward a vanishing point, in the
sense of Renaissance perspective, but on the contrary (and in absolute denial
of this doctrine) by the creation of forces in the sense of push and pull"
(Hunter 1982: 14).

As Edward Carpenter, writing for *Industrial Design*, observed, the objects
in the house "add texture, form space, and play with light that comes subtly
with constant change, through the house's transparent and translucent
shell" (Carpenter 1979: 12). This purposeful arrangement of the objects and
emphasis on their visual arrangement strip the objects of their content and
original context. Each diverse object is transformed in the interior design
into an abstract visual component of a complex formalist composition. As
a result, each item is not merely on display, it purposely works to activate
the interior perspective, transforming it into the three-dimensional visual
equivalent of Hofmann's space that "vibrates and resounds with color, light

and form in the rhythm of life." The planes, lines, texture, pattern, and colors of all the interior components, including the "functioning decoration," all play their role in this continual "push and pull" of the space. As John Neuhart recognized: "This visual richness was not decoration, or icing on the cake, but part of the cake which developed organically of the ingredients in the mix" (J. and M. Neuhart 1994: 10).

The façade and grid-like structure of the house can also be seen as representing Hofmann's "first lines" against which the constant interplay of forces occurs. The couple's enormous effort to site the building did seem to intensify this effect (Figure 3.2). The line of eucalyptus trees bordering the house was so close to it that one could not get a view of the front of the house without the trees. These trees, therefore, become an integral part of the building's design and the strict, somewhat minimalist façade thus becomes a screen (or canvas) against which one sees the movement of these trees and their play of shadows. An open meadow surrounds the house, which was only cut once a year to allow a framed view of a profusion of wild flowers and grasses, and this contrast between nature and industrially fabricated building components sets up another layer of movement. The vertical lines of the linen drapes and glimpses of the plants and furnishings that can be seen through the parts of the wall that are punctuated by transparent panels add to the complexity of the view. Instead of being static and rigid as the elevation of the façade may appear in a drawing, it together with its many screens and layers is organic, and constantly moving when one actually sees it. The house's constant interaction with nature and lighting as well as its dynamic interior design give one the impression that the building is not a static, autonomous, object but an integral component of a changing, and living space. As such, it again reflects Hofmann's theory that "space is not a static, inert thing. Space is alive; space is dynamic; space is imbued with movement expressed by forces and counterforces, space vibrates and resounds with color, light and form in the rhythm of life. Life does not exist without movement and movement does not exist without life. Movement is the expression of life" (J. and M. Neuhart 1994).

The imprint of Hans Hofmann's theories of vision is stamped clearly on the design of the Eames House.

At the same time, ideas that parallel and reflect the new "language of vision" being proposed by György Kepes, who was the Eameses' friend and colleague can also be seen. Kepes, a native of Hungary, studied painting until he emigrated to Berlin in the 1930s to collaborate on film, exhibitions, and graphic design with Laszlo Moholy-Nagy, one of the principals at the Bauhaus. Kepes followed Moholy-Nagy to London then to the United States in 1937 where he became the head of the Light and Color Department of the New Bauhaus in Chicago under his friend's direction. After the closing of the new

Bauhaus, Kepes joined the faculty at MIT in 1946 as associate professor of visual design, becoming a full professor in 1949 and institute professor in 1970. He founded the Center for Advanced Visual Studies (CAVS) in 1967 and served as its director until 1972. After Moholy-Nagy died of leukemia in 1946, Kepes expanded the exploration of "a new vision" proposed in Moholy-Nagy's books *The New Vision* (1928, 1947) and *Vision in Motion* (1947) as well as in his own pivotal study The *Language of Vision* (1944) and other various writings, particularly his *Vision and Value* series of the 1970s. The ideas put forward in *Language of Vision*, which outlined the rationale and need for a new way of seeing, form the central nucleus of Kepes's life study and teaching. For Kepes, vision was "basic to understanding, ordering and negotiating our world" (Kepes 1965: 1), but at the same time he believed that the visual richness of the contemporary world has been "diminished by artifice, superficiality and chaos, that hides true meaning." Kepes speculated that modern humankind is "undernourished" perhaps even "injured emotionally and intellectually" by this environment (Kepes 1965). He therefore suggested that vision needed to be re-trained to negotiate, enjoy, and edit the contemporary world and to "regain the health of our creative faculties, especially our visual sensibilities" (Kepes 1965). He stated: "The language of vision, optical communications, is one of the strongest potential means both to reunite man and his knowledge and to re-form into an integrated being" (Kepes 1944: 12). According to Kepes, the job of enabling this new language of vision falls naturally to both artists and designers who create new forms that can facilitate this process. His text outlines in detail the devices and techniques this new language with visual examples taken from art and graphic design in such categories as "plastic organization," "external and internal forces," "spatial tension," "dynamic equilibrium," "transparency," "interpenetration," "light and color," and "the psychological process of making." Frederick Logan in his book on reforms in art education, *Growth in American Schools*, calls Kepes's *Language of Vision* "the most important book of the 1940s and 1950s on the problems of sense perception and expression in contemporary art and design" (Golec 2002: 3).

Kepes's theories were highlighted in *Arts and Architecture* magazine, which published articles by him in 1948, 1950, and 1955. He shared a seat on the editorial advisory board of the periodical with Ray Eames at the same time that Charles Eames was an editorial associate. In an interview with Ruth Bowman in 1980, Ray Eames emphasized the importance of the magazine to her and her husband: "We were so interested in the magazine … he [John Entenza, its editor] was so interested in what it could do" (Bowman 1980: 6). Although their first meeting was not documented, the Eames and Kepes became acquainted with each other through the magazine and their published work. Correspondence in the Eames archive dating from the 1960s indicates that by that time they had become close friends who considered each other with the highest esteem.[2] Charles Eames makes numerous references to Kepes in his notes for various lectures given around the world in his lifetime, including the Eliot Norton series at Harvard in 1970–71. He mentions *Language of Vision* as a "landmark" that serves to reinforce "the value of visual presentations" (C. Eames, Eames Archive, Box 217, folder 10). By 1974, the phrase had become a way to describe his own mode of creating films and exhibitions as outlined in his article "Language of Vision: The Nuts and Bolts," in the October, 1974, issue of *The Bulletin of the American Academy of Arts and Letters* (C. Eames 1974: 18–19). In his Frank Nelson Doubleday lectures at the Smithsonian Institute in 1977, Eames seems to have co-opted the term "language of vision" for himself, using it consistently as a major subcategory of topics he thought were crucial for design and design education.

In his *Language of Vision*, Kepes theorizes that although technology and scientific discoveries had transformed the ability to see in an expansive and dynamic way (microscope, telescope, X-ray, high-speed travel) it had also created a sense of alienation in contemporary society because vision had not been educated to deal with this new way of seeing. Kepes believed that this alienation could be overcome by a reintegration of vision with the other senses, as well as with the emotions and intellect that could facilitate art and design: "To function in his fullest scope man must restore the unity of his experiences so that he can register sensory, emotional and intellectual dimensions of the present in an indivisible whole" (Kepes, *Language of Vision*, 13). Like Hofmann, Kepes envisioned the creation of new art forms relevant to humankind's contemporary situation that would function in accordance with the dynamic continuity of modern Einsteinian space-time reality as well as reflecting it. This new vision would cure humankind's alienation by providing "a perceptual experience which is dynamic and integrative (so that) the individual may awaken his anesthetized senses and emotions to achieve a recognition and active acceptance of the rich potential of the modern environment" (Marguardt 1970: 4). Similar to Hofmann as well, Kepes parallels the dynamism of the pictorial world with the real world. He defines vision as a cognitive act that "link[s] the outer vision that explores the external world with the inner vision that shapes our felt experiences into symbols" (Kepes 1960: 3). For Kepes, vision, particularly the perception of a creative art form or design, is an integrative process by which people may come to emotional terms with the complexities of the external world.

Essential to Kepes's ideas about both understanding and creating a new vision is the study of structure. "It is imperative to understand the principles of structure," he stated in an article he wrote for *Arts and Architecture*, because "creative experience may be interpreted as the 'organizer' of human capacities" (Kepes 1948). Taking the lead from studies in Gestalt psychology Kepes noted that "psychological events do not occur through accumulation of individual sense date but through the coordinated functioning of clearly pattern networks of sensation determined by structural laws" (Kepes 1956: 205). In the act of seeing, particularly "pattern-seeing," "we do not refer everything to our narrow subjective life. We trace the interplay of processes in the world" (Kepes 1956: 205). Through new vision expanding technology, one can view a "new landscape" that discloses the underlying structure and patterns of reality. Study of the structural patterns of nature can make the viewer aware of the interconnections among all organic processes. Creating new visual fields, which replicate the structural symmetries, dynamic equilibrium, rhythms, periodicity, organicism, scale relationships, and interdependence of nature, will facilitate not only a new vision, but also a new understanding and comfort with the contemporary world.

Both Charles and Ray Eames shared Kepes's preoccupation with vision and re-visioning as well as his emphasis on pattern making and structure. From Charles's early architectural works, which are referred to by Kirkham as attempts to create "totally integrated works of art," to their famous films and exhibition designs the Eameses' concern with visual organization, language, and communication is always prominent. From as early as 1945 the Eameses were already experimenting with their own visual language in such a work as "Slide Show: Lecture #1" the first of many "fast-cut" slide shows in which a sequence of a multitude of single images was projected simultaneously with a verbal or musical accompaniment. This method was later translated to the numerous film and exhibits design projects completed by the Eames Office. In an interview with Kirkham in 1983, Ray Eames related their interest in vision in these early projects: "The idea was to show how you see things. This is what it was all about—communicating visual delight in objects, through slides at first. This idea of seeing things." This approach can also be seen even in the more functional and seemingly pragmatic projects done by the office such as their furniture and interior designs. The presentations, photographs, and drawings of each piece of furniture and interior developed by the Eames Office reflect ideas and principles put forward by Kepes as a new expanded vision. For example, it became standard practice for the Eames to show an exploded view of a piece of furniture in which its parts are carefully arranged into a new pattern. Herbert Matter, the Swiss photographer and graphic designer, whose work was illustrated in Kepes's Language of Vision and was employed by the Eames in 1946, perhaps introduced this approach to presentation.[3] A photomontage of the various components of Eames furniture for Charles Eames's one-person show at the MoMA and stroboscopic images of the movement of the chairs in a tumbler designed to test their durability were created by Matter as part of the documentation of the show (Figure 3.4). These kinetic images directly echo earlier experiments in light-based and kinetic art carried on by both Moholy-Nagy and György Kepes. Charles and Ray

FIGURE 3.4 *Furniture Tumbler (left) and Stroboscopic Images (right), 1946. (Courtesy of the Eames Office, © 2018 Eames Office, LLC, eamesoffice.com, Photo: Herbert Matter).*

Eames's numerous documentation photographs of their furniture and interiors continually demonstrate this same strategy of "re-viewing" the furniture by taking it apart and regrouping the parts in new compositions, repeating its forms over and over again, or creating structured arrangements of total groups of furniture and accessories composed together. Kepes's documentation of the structure of a snowflake included in his book *The New Landscape in Art and Science*, for example, shows a marked resemblance to the aerial view shot of a table and chairs by Charles Eames (Figure 3.5). The many so-called tablescapes created by them and documented in photographs taken by the Eames of objects in their home, which emphasize structural relationships, show similar concerns.

The Eameses' method of actively engaging the eye and mind by the expanding and contracting a viewpoint from microcosm to macrocosm, as beautifully demonstrated in their movie *Powers of Ten*, also reflects concepts from Kepes's *Language of Vision*. *Powers of Ten* (1968) is a training tool that educates the contemporary eye on the possibilities of new vision that science facilitates by presenting a delightful visual journey in which the viewer is immersed in an understanding of the structural similarities and interconnectedness of life, from the smallest possible to the largest possible scale. By using a continuous zoom that takes the viewer from a picnic on

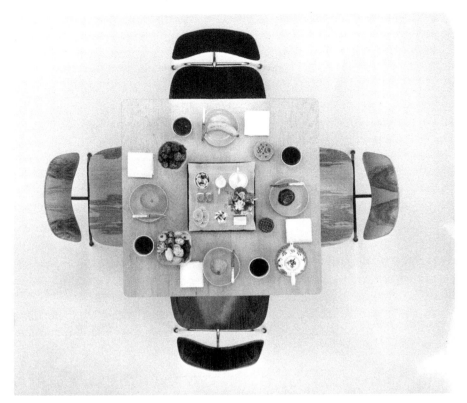

FIGURE 3.5 *Photograph of Eames Furniture. (Courtesy of Eames Office, © 2018 Eames Office, LLC (eamesoffice.com), Photo: Charles Eames).*

planet Earth out into the remote reaches of space and then back to the level of a nucleus of a carbon atom at a rate of one power of ten every ten seconds, the movie permits viewers to participate in the new vision that technology facilitates. In Kepes's *The New Landscape in Art and Science*, semiotician and philosopher Charles W. Morris describes in his essay "Man-Cosmos Symbols" that one should "look from below and above, to be inside and outside simultaneously. They can minister in this way to the strange and deep need of man to be great while being small and to remain small while becoming great" (Morris, "Man-Cosmos Symbols" in Kepes, *New Landscape,* 99). By literally demonstrating the different worlds one can navigate through enhancement or communication of one's scale, *Powers of Ten* works to bring viewers to a state of reintegration and understanding of the visual environment—a position that Kepes advocates.

Kepes's concepts achieve a similar effect to the one created in the Eames house by the use of Hofmann's push/pull as this book has suggested. At the Eames house push/pull is accomplished by arranging objects in different sizes in ascending and descending scale in relation to one another and as in relation to their disruption and activation of the visual field through a purposeful relation of objects throughout the space. Coming into the Eames house one first experiences the openness of the space, almost at the same time the eye is drawn to the numerous objects in the space, which cause viewers to refocus. Viewers are then compelled to come closer to see the smaller objects to understand their meaning and details. Small details in the objects themselves draw viewers into closer focus. Reflections, odd juxtapositions of objects, varieties of textures, and the push/pull of the visual experience of the space and objects work in tandem to cause the eye to shift back and forth dynamically from microcosm to macrocosm and back again in a similar manner to the visual journey that *Powers of Ten* creates. Looking from the interior through the large expanses of glass shifts the vision of the viewer of the Eames house again. The view of nature beyond, the play of light from the outside, and the reflections on the glass create what Kepes would call a "dialectic of artificial and natural world" (Kepes 1966: 273.). Moreover, this view exhibits the visual characteristics of transparency, overlapping, and dynamic tension that Kepes proposes as qualities of his new language of vision (Figure 3.6).

At the same time, because the house contains a variety of objects, from various cultures and various uses, one's experience of them shifts views from century to century and culture to culture while demonstrating

FIGURE 3.6 *Reflections on the Exterior of the Eames House. (Courtesy of the Eames Office, © 2018 Eames Office, LLC, eamesoffice.com. Photo: Leslie Schwartz, 2013).*

their interconnectedness and similarities of structure through their visual arrangements. In doing so it echoes Kepes sentiments: "An architect who conceives a living spatial form that can give to shelter a wider meaning enriches the language of space. Their particular language, the language of organic relatedness, helps to establish the vital continuity between the experiences of the past and present, and also ties together people living in the various corners of the globe"(Kepes 1948). The house thus provides the same educational and integrative visual experience prescribed by Kepes in order to bring human beings more in touch with their contemporary world, their fellow human beings, and themselves. Through exploring the visual language of the Eames interior, the viewer receives a better understanding of interconnections as well as a sense of delight, wonder, and excitement about the new vision that Kepes wished to engender. As Kepes scholar, Virginia Marquardt explains: "Through an active reception of an art form man may experience an organic integration, which awakens his sense and emotions to an active affirmation of the self. With his newfound identity and sense of self-worth, the individual may more openly participate in social interaction and thereby overcome his alienation from his fellow man" (Marquardt 1970: 39). Like Hofmann, Kepes also proposed a state of "dynamic equilibrium" as an ideal. Marquardt writes:

> Given the conflict between order and chaos, the intellect and the emotions, the artist must seek a dynamic equilibrium by which the viewer can grasp the structured rhythm yet maintain an interest in the variety of visual relationships which are purposefully directed and ordered. Dynamic equilibrium can be defined as a stable phenomenon composed of ever changing and unpredictable variation. (Marquardt 1970: 66)

This idea is also apparent in the house's design. Even as the structural rational order of the house emulates Hofmann's "first lines," it can also be seen in terms of Kepes's concept of "static order" against which a balance of "chaotic change" can take place to create the "dynamic continuity," a characteristic of his new visual language and a means for making a design or piece of artwork vital. As Kepes states in *Language of Vision:* "If the image is to remain a living organism, the relationships within it must have progressively changing aspects" (Kepes 1944: 59). For the Eames the enlargement of vision and the viewer's self-conscious interaction with their environment was essential for self-fulfillment: "If people would only realize," Charles Eames said, "that they have the real stuff right in their hand, in their back yards, their lives would be richer. They are afraid to get involved. That's why they call in decorators, because they are afraid. To do their own decorating they have to get themselves involved in thinking and feeling" (Davenport 1962: 27).

This dynamic ever-changing perspective embedded in the design of the Eames House and reflective of a concern with the new vision espoused by both Hofmann and Kepes would later be manifested in all the Eameses' work. In the Exhibition of Modern Living held at Detroit Institute of Arts in 1949, the exhibition's curator Alexander Girard invited Alvar Aalto, Florence Knoll, Bruno Mathesson, George Nelson, Jens Risom, Eero Saarinen, and the Eameses to create exhibits for objects they designed. George Nelson described the Eames room in this show as "not so much a literal presentation of a room as the expression of an attitude conveyed through the use of a special personal vocabulary." In 1950 their design for the Herman Miller Showroom in Los Angeles, for the inaugural exhibition space for the Good Design shows in Chicago, windows for Carson Pirie Scott, and for a home for film director Billy Wilder all allowed the Eameses to showcase the same application of Hofmann's principles of push/pull through the careful placements of items of different scales and origins and the visual primacy and balancing act that the interior design of their own home demonstrated. Pictures that document the working environment of their office 901 Washington Blvd. in Venice, CA and particularly the film created to record its closing and deconstruction after Ray's death in 1988, *901: After 45 Years of Working* shows clearly the imprint of the of their "language of vision" and the incorporation of a "dynamic equilibrium" within the plethora of parts and possessions that constructed that environment. The new language of vision that their associates Hofmann and Kepes both separately propounded definitively resonated and perhaps shaped the Eameses' personal vocabulary of interior design. Unfortunately for the field, while the Eameses continued their investigation of this vocabulary in the various exhibition design and movies that they created in the 1950, '60s, and '70s, they undertook no major architectural commissions after 1951 because they were frustrated by their lack of control in building projects. Nonetheless, the Eames House provided a prime example of how the dynamics of a new way of seeing could bring richness and humanity to the interior environment. As the commentary to their design for the "Design for Modern Living" at the Detroit Institute of Art in 1949 points out, the "'Eames' basic approach to modern design ... suggests that the enjoyment of any two objects is increased . proportionately by their proper relation to each other" (Kaufmann jr. 1949: 81).

Although its theoretical basis may not be understood, their dynamic visual approach to interior design was greatly emulated by their contemporaries and continues to remain influential in interior design today when their house is lauded as "one of the world's most significant modern residences" (Makovsky 2004).

Parts of this chapter were first published in Lucinda Kaukas Havenhand (2006) "American Abstract Art and the Interior Design of Ray and Charles Eames," *Journal of Interior Design*, 31:2, 29–42 and are reused here with permission of John Wiley & Sons, Inc.

4

George Nelson:
Humanism, Morality,
and the Japanese Aesthetic

While Ray and Charles Eames may be the best-known designers from the mid-century modern period, many people might not know the name George Nelson. This is because in his position of design director at Herman Miller Furniture Company the company's name always took precedence over his. Well-known and well-used designs like Nelson's platform bench, still produced by Herman Miller are found all over our visual landscape in interiors of many kinds, but may not be recognized as Nelson's in the same way and Eames chairs are. This is ironic since George Nelson from his position as editor for *Architectural Forum*, design director for the Herman Miller Company, and head of his own firm in New York City played an essential and leading role in the development of modern design in the United States. Although Nelson is often labeled as an industrial designer and theorist, he thought of himself a "universal" designer who worked in all aspects of design and had a strong impact on interior design in the 1940s and '50s. Most importantly Nelson was a dedicated humanist—a man interested in ideas, behavior, and the inner and outer workings of human beings—who spent his long career considering how design could be used to support the human condition. A close study of George Nelson, particularly his interiors for the Herman Miller Company, reveals that as a design/scholar/writer Nelson explored many ideas throughout his lifetime, delighted in analysis about what he learned and speculated constantly about how design related to them. Of any of the designers considered in this study he was the strongest theorist who used both design and words to express and explore his speculations. Nelson's lifelong study of humanistic theories, particularly the work of Erich Fromm, José Ortega y Gasset, and Alfred North Whitehead, combined with his interest in Japanese aesthetics, allowed him to create a model for a more humane, moral, and life-enhancing approach to interior design and in doing so provided one of the best examples for interior designers of how to translate theory into design practice.

The path to modern design

George Nelson was born into an upper-middle-class household to parents who introduced him early to culture and learning and imbued him with his strong understanding of the importance of intellectual inquiry. Nelson later went on to be trained in architecture, receiving a BFA from Yale in 1931. Soon after graduating, he won the Prix de Rome and traveled to the American Academy to study for two years. There he was exposed to percolating developments in modern architecture and was able to meet and interview many prominent architects of the day. Nelson had received a traditional Beaux-Arts education at Yale so his decision to practice in the modern idiom when he set up an architectural practice with William Hamby in New York City in 1936 was most likely the result of this experience. Nelson received his first major recognition as a designer in 1945 when an idea called *Storagewall*, developed in partnership with architect Henry Wright, was given an eight-page layout in *Life* magazine, which featured a pictorial before-and-after that demonstrated how the product could modernize any home. This concept of "built-in" storage promoted by Nelson was soon identified as an essential feature of the modern home in the postwar period and brought him into a national spotlight as a designer. The *Storagewall* article most importantly brought Nelson to the attention of D.J. DePree, then president of the Herman Miller Furniture Company. As one of the few manufacturers of modern furniture during the 1930s and '40s, the Herman Miller Company was experiencing moderate success when its director of design Gilbert Rohde died in 1944. Committed to continuing the production of modern furniture, DePree pursued George Nelson as Rohde's replacement. DePree was reportedly impressed with his "fertile mind, design awareness, and ability to articulate important principles" (C. and K. Fehrmann 1987: 28) and offered him the position. Nelson openly admitted he knew nothing about furniture design but accepted the job. His intellectual spark in combination with his design sensibility and talent seems to have compensated for his lack of direct knowledge of furniture production and he remained design director for Herman Miller for over twenty years. In addition to his furniture and built-in storage, Nelson made many other contributions during the postwar period that were influential in shaping its modern design aesthetic. His track lighting and "Bubble" lamps, created for the Howard Miller Company in the 1950s, were among the first modern, inexpensive lighting fixtures available. He also brought the American public an early version of the portable television tray table and reinvented the concept of keeping time with his numberless wall and alarm clocks. He created new lines of plastic dishes, fireplace accessories, and vertical blinds, and translated most of the accouterments of daily life into a modern style. Architect Michael Graves, who worked in the Nelson office from 1959 to 1960, called Nelson "the consummate modernist" (Abercrombie 2000: 29).

Nelson's verbal and writing skills enabled him to also become a prolific spokesperson about modern design in the postwar period. He began his career as a critic and theorist of modern design when as a student at the American Academy in Rome in the 1930s he was hired by the magazine *Pencil Points* (the precursor of *Progressive Architecture*) to write a series of articles on contemporary European architecture. Nelson's twelve articles entitled "The Architects of Europe Today," published from 1935 to 1936, provided readers in the United States some of the first generally available information on modern European architecture. The success of these articles established Nelson's reputation as a writer, and in 1935 he was invited to become associate editor for *Architectural Forum* and *Fortune* magazines. In 1944, he was made head of *Fortune-Forum*'s experimental division and was a contributing editor to *Interiors* magazine from 1948 to 1956 and wrote regularly for both *Interior Design* and *Industrial Design* magazines. During his lifetime he was the author of nearly two hundred articles and the editor of many more. In 1945, he collaborated with architect Henry Wright to author *Tomorrow's House*, an instructive text used as a reference guide for those wishing to modernize their homes in the 1940s and '50s. In the 1950s, Nelson published three books—*Living Spaces, Chairs,* and *Storage*—that were collections of various designs of the period and included texts by Nelson on each of these subject areas. A series of essays (most originally published as individual articles in such magazines as *Interiors*) were first published in book form in 1957 as *Problems of Design*. In the late 1970s, Nelson compiled two more collections of his essays: *How to See: Visual Adventures in a World God Never Made* (1977) and *George Nelson on Design* (1979). More anecdotal and philosophical than his early accounts, these volumes reflect and summarize the various experiences and methodologies that affected his designs throughout his career. Nelson also played an influential role in the field of design education. He was invited to lecture at Harvard, Columbia, University of Georgia, University of Michigan, and UCLA at various times in his career and to give talks throughout the world, including playing an active role in the International Design Conference held yearly in Aspen, Colorado.

George Nelson's interest in modern design originates more in his writings and travels than in his architectural training. While a Prix de Rome winner and later when contracted by *Pencil Points* magazine to write about modern architecture Nelson traveled throughout Europe documenting the architectural landscape in numerous sketches and notes. He was a talented draftsman whose drawing skills brought him many early accolades, but by the postwar period Nelson had abandoned sketching to use photography as his primary documentation tool—a device he would use all his life and to fill his later books and articles with images. While traveling Nelson began his first discussions and documentations of modern design. He wrote: "In Rome, the extraordinary thing I learned was that everything was modern ... everything that is worth anything is always modern because it can't be anything else ... you just do the thing you can honestly do now" (Nelson 1979: 15). Since he had been trained in a traditional Beaux Arts approach to architecture at Yale, the emerging International Style architecture that he encountered in Europe provided him with new lessons in his design education. Nelson essentially had as his teachers, the twelve architects he chose to write about in his articles including prominent early modernists, such as Walter Gropius, Le Corbusier, and Mies van der Rohe. These lessons had a great impact on Nelson, and on returning to the United States from Europe he began to promote the development of the modern design particularly from his position as a writer and later an editor for *Architectural Forum* and *Interiors* magazines. In October 1937, he helped produce a special issue of *Architectural Forum* on the modern domestic interior, which focused on five designers: Ernest Born, Richard Neutra, Gilbert Rohde, Eero Saarinen, and Russel Wright. Nelson wrote the introduction for the issue, which advocated for the functionalist modernist approach being demonstrated by these designers. He also brought the traditional/modern debate to the foreground in an exhibition he designed for the Architectural League of New York called "Versus" in 1940, which compared the conservative historical approach with the progressive modern one and allowed him an audience for his pro-modern views.

By 1941, Nelson was able to put modern concepts into practice in his own interior design in the Fairchild House in New York City done in collaboration with his then partner William Hamby. The building was featured in *The New Yorker*'s column "Talk of the Town," in 1941, which reported on its use of modern elements such as ramps instead of staircases, a glass walled interior courtyard and electrically operated venetian blinds. The house reveals the impact that a number of European designers had on the young Nelson in its stripped down horizontal façade, open plan, and reliance on materials as structure and decoration. Since Nelson had not yet started his furniture design career, however, the house was mostly furnished in upholstered furniture and decorative lighting fixtures that still retained some historical associations, a problem he would soon remedy when he went to work for Herman Miller. In a photograph of Nelson's design for his office at *Fortune* magazine in 1945 (Figure 4.1), one can see indications of the modern approach to the interior that he would promote in his first catalog for Herman Miller published the

FIGURE 4.1 *George Nelson, Office at Fortune Magazine, 1945. (© Vitra Design Museum, George Nelson Estate. Photo: Elmer L. Astleford).*

next year. In this office, his own specifically designed modern furniture is integrated with the architecture and contributes to a sleek, minimal, non-decorative, and mostly horizontal space that combines natural and industrial materials with broad unembellished expanses of color. The custom design of the venetian blinds, a variety of small drawers for specific supplies and tools on the desk, and the lighting reflect European design's concern for functional detail as well as its influence on Nelson. In 1949 Nelson participated in "An Exhibition on Modern Living" curated by designer Alexander Girard for the Detroit Institute of Art (Figure 4.2). Nelson designed one room that allowed him to investigate more fully his concept of a totally modern interior. In this model room Nelson created a functional, integrated space, which incorporates seating with built-in cabinets that house a desk, bookshelves, storage, lighting, and entertainment equipment. In his catalog essay MoMA curator Edgar Kaufmann jr. commented on Nelson's integrative functional approach to the design: "In this room, George Nelson admirably develops his thesis that, as much as possible, furniture should be included *within* the design and construction of the room itself. Here ... is a comfortable, well-equipped living area in which the furniture is confined to two light chairs and small sofa-table—everything else being built-in" (Girard and Laurie 1949: 27). In these early designs, Nelson created interiors that were visually recognizable as modern and emphatically functional. In a 1937 issue of *Architectural Forum* dedicated to interior design, he outlined his reasoning behind them:

FIGURE 4.2 *George Nelson, Model Room for "An Exhibition on Modern Living,"
1949. (© Vitra Design Museum, George Nelson Estate).*

Our environment contains the stuff for creating new backgrounds and changing the old. The pressure of modern existence, as much as anything, killed the overstuffed interior, and while the monastic cell is no solution, the requirements of daily life must be provided for before decoration is considered ... the functional approach is basic and provides the framework for this issue.

Humanism, philosophy, and George Nelson

While George Nelson was an early and ardent promoter of a functional modernism, he was also one of the first designers to consider its shortcomings. As early as the late 1940s one can also see that while remaining an advocate for modern design, Nelson began to be concerned about the direction it was taking. Nelson's biographer, Stanley Abercrombie, notes that by 1942, when Nelson was hired to teach night school at Columbia University, "Modernism ... was in full sway ... but in a stylistically orthodox manner that Nelson had already come to view as restrictive and monotonous" (Abercrombie 2000: 28). Nelson was concerned about the de-humanizing effect of strictly formulaic approaches to designing. Abercrombie relates that Nelson kept notebooks all his life in which he recorded quotes from various sources. In one notebook he made a notation taken from the architect and typographer Eric Gill's autobiography written in 1940 that reflects this particular concern: "The whole thing [business of contemporary architecture] is completely inhuman. And the result is what anyone might expect but few people see—a world in which buildings are not only dead but damned" (Gill 1940: 111). When one records or underlines parts of a text written by another author it is often because it resonates with the reader and is reflective of a shared like-mindedness. One can easily speculate in this manner about the passages recorded in the Nelson notebooks, since quotes like these and others relate directly to the developing themes of his designs and writings about modern design. The Gill quotation reflects an ongoing thread through all of Nelson work by the 1940s: saving modern design from its being destroyed by standardized functional and technological approaches that drain life and beauty from it. Nelson demonstrated a lifelong concern that consumerism, and particularly technology, could not only devalue, but ultimately lead to the destruction of humankind. Like his mentor and friend, Erich Fromm,[1] Nelson was intrigued with humans' destructive tendencies and the collaborative role design might play in affecting them. He was well aware of these deadly potentials and wrote about them (albeit somewhat sarcastically) in articles such as "How to Kill: A Problem of Design," a diatribe about how design had made the ability to kill so efficient. Amid the looming tensions of the Cold War era, Nelson saw design as having the potential to both help destroy and save the world and using design to help facilitate a safer, saner, richer, and more humane world became a lifelong preoccupation. In an article written in 1973, he summarized his concern for a humanistic approach to modern design that became the focus of his career as a designer:

> I cannot believe that the creative role for the designer *now* can be anything other than the production of humane environments. Anything else, given the social context, is anachronistic, inconsequential, egotistical and empty posturing.
>
> The real problem for the designer is not only to find clients: *he must first determine what a humane environment really is.* The answers are not available in the supermarket. What seems to be needed is observation, study, interdisciplinary friction and thought, directed towards the creation of a new cultural base, which is an indispensable prerequisite for a revised set of social priorities.
>
> The human environment is not a slogan: it is a mystery, which can only be penetrated by humane people. (Nelson 1973: 511)

George Nelson believed that "those who preach progressive ideas must practice them,"[2] and developed an approach to design that consistently did incorporate "observation, study, interdisciplinary friction and thought" and that allowed him to explore, "interior design principles that transcended specific installations" (Abercrombie 2000: 38). Nelson's "interdisciplinary friction, study and thought" came from a variety of diverse sources that he noted in his writings and notebooks, ranging from the study of ancient cultures to the field of astrophysics. His lifelong avoidance of classifying himself within the realm of only one profession reflected his advocacy of the need for an interdisciplinary approach. As early as his stay in Europe during his Prix de Rome years, he speculated on the need to be a "universal" designer—one concerned with the broader issues of society who was not limited by the tunnel vision of vocational categories. While still in Europe, he wrote:

> If the architect could get away from the specialization that has characterized the profession in recent years, if he could once more set out confidently as the universal designer, if he could correlate all of his experience in handling form with his training in the matter of logically combining and expressing complicated functions, he would fill an extremely important place that no one at the present time is better qualified to occupy. (Nelson 1936: 133)

Nelson never limited himself to one occupational label during his lifetime, and contributed to a variety of disciplines, often working on many levels and in many roles in his projects. But if one wished to summarize Nelson at all, perhaps the most appropriate label would be that of philosopher, for his lifelong love of learning and desire to better understand himself and his world exemplifies Whitehead's definition of a philosopher as one who attempts "to express the infinity of the universe in terms of the limitations of language" (Schilpp 1951: 14). In Nelson's case, his language was not only the written word, but also design—a visual and physical language that can be applied to all aspects of life. From an overview of both Nelson's writings and those about him, one can discern that his study of philosophical theories informs his aspirations to be a universal designer as well as his designs. Nelson's writings reveal that three major thinkers inspired or supported his efforts during the postwar years. In typical Nelson fashion these sources are diverse: the work of an English Protestant, Alfred North Whitehead; a Spanish Catholic, José Ortega y Gasset; and a German Jew, Eric Fromm (who would later introduce him to the work of a Japanese Buddhist, Daisetz T. Suzuki).

Alfred North Whitehead (1861–1947) was a philosopher and mathematician of Nelson's grandfather's generation, most noted for his work with Bertrand Russell in developing the three-volume treatise *Principia Mathematica*, but who was awarded a teaching appointment in philosophy at Harvard University in 1931 where he focused on metaphysics more than math. Whitehead's philosophical work centers around the theme that process, rather than substance, is the fundamental metaphysical constituent of the world. He believed that if philosophers were to understand truly the nature of reality then they needed to make connections between objective and rational descriptions of the world and the more emotive and personal realm of subjective experience. In his writings and speeches Nelson quotes frequently from Whitehead's *Aims of Education* written in 1929; his aphorism "Style is the ultimate morality of the mind," was reportedly one of Nelson's favorites. Nelson also quoted José Ortega y Gasset's (1883–1955) *The Revolt of the Masses* (1930) and *History as a System* (1939) throughout his career. Notable Ortega quotes, such as "To be surprised, to wonder, is to begin to understand" from *Revolt of the Masses* and "Today I am more than ever frightened. I wish it would dawn upon engineers that, in order to be an engineer, it is not enough to be an engineer" from *Man the Technician* (Ortega y Gasset 1941: 103) obviously resonated with Nelson's need to be intellectually vigorous as well as his reluctance to limit himself within one profession. Stanley Abercrombie describes a meeting between Nelson and William Dunlap, president of Aluminum Manufacturing Company, with whom Nelson was conducting business in 1949. Dunlap recalls that at their first meeting, "we talked of philosophy, poetry and almost every esoteric subject except design and aluminum" (Abercrombie 2000: 121). Dunlap said that Ortega y Gasset was one of Nelson's favorite writers and that the designer presented him with a copy of *The Revolt of the Masses* as a token of their friendship (Abercrombie 2000: 122). Ortega deplored the development of the "mass-man" and of "mass-mind" which he felt both numbed and degraded the human condition. Nelson referred to Ortega y Gasset's theories often, as in his article "Reflections on *Home-Psych*" in *Interior Design* magazine in March 1984, where he discussed his theory of mass culture in detail to explain mass trends in interior design. In the article, Nelson explains that:

> By "masses" he [Ortega] does not mean any of the familiar categories, such as commoners versus aristocrats, or workers versus professionals or management. For Ortega there are only two kinds of people, "those who make great demands on themselves ... and those who demand nothing special for themselves ... mere buoys that float on the waves." (Nelson 1984)

Nelson identified himself clearly as one of those "who makes great demands on themselves," and aspired to be one of Ortega's "noble men" who impacted the world in a positive way through his efforts.

The third philosophical influence on Nelson was that of his contemporary, the psychologist and personality theorist, Erich Fromm. Fromm studied the psychological theories of Freud in Germany in the 1920s and '30 and developed his own more sociological approach to psychoanalysis in the '40s after immigrating to America. Nelson asked Fromm to be a consultant for a new magazine he was developing for Time-Life after the publication of his bestselling book *Escape from Freedom* in 1940. Later Nelson became his patient and lifelong friend. Abercrombie relates that a notebook of Nelson's contained a dozen pages labeled "Fromm" that constitute quickly written notes that may have recorded his discussions with Fromm or his lectures and confirm "a teacher/student relationship beyond the usual analyst/analysee relationship" (Abercrombie 2000: 330). Nelson often refers to Fromm's major premise that there are two opposing approaches to existence—"having" and "being"—and that the having mode, based in aggression and greed, promoted the accumulation of material possessions while being, based in love, emphasized shared experience and productive activity.

Although Nelson's inspiration comes from diverse sources, the works of these three men share commonalities that Nelson recognized and also practiced. The first is their interest in intellectual inquiry as well as humanistic concerns. All held the common belief that in order to be fully human being one must continuously search for meaning in life. Ortega referred to this as the effort of "the noble man", Fromm the process of "loving" and "being," and

Whitehead, the job of the philosopher, one's highest avocation. Each of these men's speculations on the meaning of life took various paths, but they all shared the conclusion that rationalism and repetitive standardized approaches could never fully describe existence or bring one an understanding of it. All three stressed the need to investigate the more subjective realms of the "mysterious," "magical," "transcendent," "noble," "adventurous," "emotional," and the "personal." All had an accessible and almost anecdotal writing style that they used to discuss these ideas that Nelson also advocated. Fromm, Ortega, and Whitehead all saw that rationality, technology, mass culture, as well as consumerism, threatened to drain the vitality from civilization and the ability of humankind to fully embrace and understand life. As Fromm stated in a quote recorded by Nelson in his notebook: "We live in a world of things, and our only connection with them is that we know how to manipulate or to consume them" (Fromm 1955: 134). He noted the similar thoughts of Ortega: "Our time, being the most intensely technical, is also the emptiest in human history" (Ortega y Gasset 1941: 151). Whitehead too was skeptical about over rationalized and scientific approaches. This sense of doubt is well expressed in his famous declaration, "Exactness is a fake" (Whitehead 1941: 700), which Whitehead scholar Henry Holmes says embodies Whitehead belief that "our sharp decisions about meanings, values, causes, and the future, as we draw them from the carefully distinguished facts of science, are less definitive than we suppose" (Schilpp 1951: 622).

Fromm, Ortega y Gasset, and Whitehead recognized that as people struggled to know their world, the world constantly changed, and therefore methods of investigation and thinking processes needed to change constantly as well. They recognized that all aspects of the world were interconnected and dynamic. Ortega posited the existential claim "I am I and my circumstances" (Ortega y Gasset 2004); Fromm developed an approach to psychoanalysis, which unlike Freud's clearly placed the individual within a social context and denied claims of an independent *a priori* self; and Whitehead posited: "Nature is a structure of evolving processes. The reality is the process" (Whitehead 1932: 90). Once again Holmes, paraphrasing Whitehead, encapsulates this shared idea best when he states that Whitehead believed that:

> The world is not a junkyard of dead stuff, known from without by consciousness, either human or divine—or both; it is a dynamic process creating itself and unity itself in a continuum to which it gives a real and differentiated content. But this process is the movement and adventuring, the never-ending birth and death, of entities far simpler than the human soul; and it finds its unity in modes of being quite beyond our finite consciousness. (Schilpp 1951: 622)

Following the path of his three mentors, Nelson developed a belief that incorporated his efforts to discover meaning and purpose in life. Throughout his work, he consistently engaged in the active process of looking, thinking, and discovering as well as applying that information to his design process. Believing that "modernism was here to stay but that it needed a symbolic soul" (Abercrombie 2000: 30), George Nelson always maintained a deeply philosophical concern for humankind and its designs. When he quotes from Whitehead's *The Aims of Education* to the effect that "Style is the ultimate morality of mind," he points to a shared belief with this philosopher that design can be an agent of transcendence, life-enhancement, and promotion of a greater good. Like his mentors, Nelson believed that meaning in life and in design was relational and dynamic. In a speech to the American Institute of Architects in 1951 he stated: "meaning, for contemporary man, resides less in the esthetic qualities of individual structures than in the tensions set up by their various relationships" (Nelson, speech to American Institute of Architects 1951). The theme of interconnection was a recurrent and persistent one in Nelson's work in all areas. In reference to an experimental art course he developed for the University of Georgia called "Art-X," Nelson explained that it was designed to make a statement that "there was no longer room in the world for barriers" and that art, "like every other discipline, is not an isolated thing but intimately related to everything in creation, including man and all his works, past, present, and future" (Nelson 1954: 149). The Italian designer Ettore Sottsass, who worked at the Nelson office in the 1950s and was a lifelong friend, noted this quality in Nelson's approach to using photography and creating photomontages:

> George's logic in choosing the photographs to be taken inevitably and exactly fitted the logic of his existential design. He went ahead by small steps, slowly but insistently digging out an image of the world around him. It was not a world that could be defined outright, not a total landscape or reality, but a world that could, if anything, be defined as a compound of dynamic links between infinite quantities of details, infinite quantities of rapid images, visible and invisible, see, foreseen, and never actually appearing, infinite surface and subterranean tensions. (Abercrombie 2000: xi)

This theme of using a dynamic perspective to create more humane designs that bring users in touch with their world persists in Nelson's career and is always evident in his writings and his designs. As Sottsass notes: "George Nelson's existential vision acknowledges no compartments, partition walls, specializations, or special keys. Life and thought, the irrational, the rational, the true and the imaginary, were for him open regions, permanent collages, continuous landscapes to be crossed" (Nelson 1954: viii). Throughout his career, Nelson set diligently upon the path of Ortega's "noble man" spending his life in Whitehead's "adventure of ideas" in search of a better understanding of his world through processes that were sometimes joyful and playful and at other times serious and critical, for the purpose of achieving Fromm's sense of "being" rather than "having." Nelson shared this adventure with the American public in both his writings and through the creation of his specific style of design that interwove humanistic concerns with modernism for the purpose of creating Whitehead's "ultimate morality of the mind."

Nelson's humanist interiors and the Japanese aesthetic

Nelson's mature design approach can be best seen in his work in the 1950s, which includes the interiors illustrated in the 1952 and 1956 reprint of the Herman Miller catalog, his designs for the inside of Buckminster Fuller's Geodesic Dome Environment (1952), his plans for an Experimental House (1951–57), as well as in his instructional writings of the period. His search for "interdisciplinary friction," as inspired by his aforementioned mentors, is clearly recognizable both in his designs and in his writings of the period. From them one can see that a major source of information and inspiration for his quest to create a more humane and vital modernism comes from his admiration and study of Japanese design. In his introduction to a book about the Japanese art of packaging, titled *How to Wrap Five Eggs* and published in 1965, he writes of his admiration for the Japanese approach: "What we have lost for sure is what this book is all about: a once-common sense use of fitness in the relationships between hand, material, use and shape, and above all, a sense of delight in the look and feel of very ordinary, humble things" (Nelson in Oka 1967). Nelson recognized that the richness of Japanese design, which was delightful as well as life enhancing, stemmed from what he would call its "honesty." Nelson recognized honesty in design as the attempt to understand the "true" nature of a material and to express that understanding in a respectful use of it. The designer's attempt to discern the essence of materials and to use them appropriately can be seen as way of trying to know the world better to bring harmony and appropriateness to design, and to create a connection between the designer, the user, and the physical world. The sense of harmony, unity, and relation to one's world created in this way then radiates out into the world like a stone dropped in a pool, generating the enhanced sense of being and interconnectedness that all his mentors advocated. Nelson believed that honest design brings a new awareness and appreciation to living as do poems, works of art, and philosophical treatises.

His study and emulation of Japanese design can be seen as a quest to bring this quality to contemporary design and is an integral part of his development of a more humane modernism.

George Nelson's interest and appreciation of Japanese design can be readily documented. He relates in his writing that he first became aware of Japanese design as early as in the fifth grade from a schoolbook entitled *Little Friends from Far and Near*. Nelson wrote that the book showed pictures of the Japanese house, which he later understood "met the requirements of Japanese daily life, economy, social tradition and climate with such exquisite appropriateness that as a design for living it had never been surpassed" (Nelson 1957: 126). In 1948 he wrote an article for *Holiday* magazine entitled "The Japanese House," which was later reprinted in his book *Problems of Design*. In this article, Nelson noted similarities and differences between Japanese and the American approaches to architecture. He took note of the parallels between the designs of modern houses and the Japanese house, commenting that "without much direct influences we have been developing a modern house in this country that bears a strong resemblance to it" (Nelson 1957: 130). He applauded the economy of means and richness of results in traditional Japanese houses and he concluded that Americans have much to gain by studying this type of house because of its naturalness, honesty, and its flexible response to human needs that make one reconsider the world in new way. He wrote:

> [The Japanese house] teaches that the beautiful way to handle materials, whether paper or wood, rock or shrub is the natural way. It suggests that you can get attention by whispering as well as shouting, that simplicity is not the same as bare emptiness, that poverty is not necessarily ugly, and that for full living people require a flexible enclosure not a straight jacket. (Nelson 1957: 131)

Nelson traveled to Japan in 1951 as part of group of designers invited after the Peace Treaty of San Francisco to help the Japanese develop new products for export, and he returned again in 1957. These trips resulted in further articles about Japanese design: one in *Print* magazine showed examples of Japanese packaging; and a syndicated column, that was published in dozens of American newspapers, was entitled "What I See," which was a visual documentation of Japanese products such as tools and housewares and a discussion of how Nelson was working on adapting these designs for American living. In 1959, his collection of Japanese advertisements, calendars, and posters was shown by the American Institute of Graphic Arts; and his article "Impressions of Japan," which was illustrated with his own photographs, was published in *Holiday* in February 1960. In this article Nelson commented: "To go to

Japan is to fall in love." He explained that "the experience was thoroughly disturbing and thoroughly healthy" and added that this disturbance was rooted in the fact that " we [the U.S.] operate on the basis of ninety percent intellect and ten percent emotion, while in Japan the proportions are exactly reversed" (Nelson 1960: 67). Nelson's interest in Japanese design as well as his concern with creating a more humane modernism was also supported by his lifelong friendship with the Japanese American architect Minoru Yamasaki. In the 1940s, Nelson and Yamasaki met when they were both teaching at Columbia University, and then considered becoming business partners at various times throughout their careers. Yamasaki went on to become famous for being involved with some now infamous design projects—the Pruitt-Igoe apartments, the modern housing blocks whose demolition is often noted as the beginning of postmodernism, and the World Trade Center's twin towers which were destroyed in the terrorist attack of 2001—but he is also known for his attempts to fuse more humanistic details into his modern buildings. In an interview with Virginia Harriman for the Archives of American Art in 1959, Yamasaki articulates how his ideas parallel those of Nelson. He related that on a recent trip he had taken around the world in 1954 he realized that "architecture as we were practicing it—not necessarily the way that I was practicing it—but the way that society was practicing it—was inadequate in a sense, and that it did not bring us the kind of experience as people that we ought to make available to ourselves" (Harriman interview with Yamasaki, 1959, Smithsonian Archives of American Art, 2). Like Nelson, Yamasaki felt that Japanese design in particular possessed qualities that American design and architecture should aspire to. This included a sense of surprise or delight, which he found that traditional Japanese architecture created through its juxtaposition of unexpected pockets of tranquility (such as Japanese gardens and temple interiors) in contrast to moments of incredible chaos (the Japanese city street). Whether Nelson and Yamasaki talked directly about these specific ideas and the model Japanese design presented for a more human modernism is not known, but the two friends clearly shared and appreciated the same concerns in their lives and work. Nelson's interest in Japanese aesthetics was most likely also enhanced by his interaction with Erich Fromm. In the early 1940s, when Nelson was entering into his friendship with Fromm, this philosopher was also beginning a close association with the famous Japanese scholar of Zen Buddhism, Daisetz T. Suzuki (Funk 2000: 133). Suzuki visited Fromm in Mexico (as did Nelson) in the 1950s. In 1957 Fromm and Suzuki held a one-week seminar that focused on joining the unconscious based with Zen principles. Suzuki and Fromm later published their findings in a co-authored book titled *Zen Buddhism and Psychoanalysis* (1960). Certainly, Nelson would have been aware of Suzuki because of his ongoing discussions with Fromm during this period.

As early as his publication of *Tomorrow's House* in 1945 one can see Nelson advocating for the search for "natural" and "honest" designs that he admired in the Japanese work. In that book he states: "The great tradition in architecture is honest building ... We have included only modern houses in this book because in our time they are the only way to carry out the great tradition" (Nelson and Wright 1945: 6–7). Nelson was convinced that modern houses carry on a tradition of "honest building" and "naturalness" because of their direct, unembellished use of materials and straightforward plans (Nelson and Wright 1945). He felt that this imbued a structure with a Whiteheadian sense of morality: "The modern house is a good house because it is a 'natural' house," he said (Nelson and Wright 1945: 102). However, not all modern approaches to interior design had the naturalness that Nelson was looking for. He found that in Mies van der Rohe's Tugendhat House, for example, that "the architect had clearly kept control of the job until the last dish had been installed on the last shelf, but as far as I could then see, the whole affair was more like a museum than a house. It had precious little to do with the habits or requirements of any family I had ever encountered" (Nelson 1957: 186). He found Frank Lloyd Wright's interiors to be better but was still critical of their sense of permanence and inflexibility: "His rooms were so designed that they seem furnished before the furniture got in, and there was the feeling that almost anything would be an unwarranted intrusion" (Nelson 1957: 187). Again and again Nelson turned to Japanese design as the best examples of a more truthful, delightful and humane modernism. He illustrated this idea in his 1948 article on the Japanese house and in other instructive polemics written over the decades. In his essay entitled "Problems of Design: Modern Decoration" (1949) he noted that "[in] the Japanese interior we have a superb instance of what takes place when the problem of interior design is attacked on the highest level: everything is simultaneously meaningful and decorative" (Nelson 1957: 191).

In the third re-printing of the Herman Miller catalog (1956) one can see Nelson incorporating these examples in the creation of spaces that are less about function, technology, and European modernism and more about their impact on users and interconnection with them. The lessons of his mentors and subsequently of his study of Japanese design are clearly in play here. Nelson's assimilation of these influences results in interior designs that are more direct, unified, simple, and strikingly elegant in their honest use of both traditional and new materials and their more delightful and life enhancing qualities. Photographs of model interiors in the 1956 version of the Herman Miller catalog (Figure 4.3) exhibit leanness and horizontality of Japanese design. The forms of both the overall composition and the individual components are stripped down in an attempt to reveal their essential qualities, but at the same time they almost paradoxically exude a warm and inviting presence. Nelson's

FIGURE 4.3 *George Nelson, Interior design (studio shot) with furniture by George Nelson from Herman Miller Collection Catalog, 1956, p. 9–10 (page gap reworked). (© Vitra Design Museum, George Nelson Estate).*

furniture during this period, including his Thin-edged bed and Rosewood series cabinets, as well as their artful arrangement in modern interiors demonstrate a regulation and geometry that reflects the ordering and sparseness as well as the richness and honesty he admired in Japanese traditional architecture.

Particularly noticeable in Nelson ensembles is the sense of space that combines stillness with the potentials for action and interaction that is also a characteristic of traditional Japanese interiors. The space and the furniture embrace the user in an intimate and human scale emphasized by the U-shaped configuration of the elements that Nelson often uses. In his 1948 article, "Problems of Design: The Dead End Room" (1948), Nelson noted that users of interiors spaces seem always to migrate and feel more comfortable in enclosed configurations. He theorizes that this tendency relates to human beings' instinctive need for protection and shelter. He incorporated this so-called "dead-end" configuration often in his 1950 interiors, integrating it also in his model interior designed for Buckminster Fuller's Geodesic dome in 1952. For this project, Nelson created cave-like pavilions that are entirely open on one side (Figure 4.4), much like a room in a Japanese house that has its exterior partition drawn back in order to view a garden. In his plan for Experimental House (1951), Nelson accentuates this sense of enclosure by creating a sunken seating area in the middle of its living room, which re-conceptualizes the Japanese custom of sitting directly on the floor into a modern form (Figure 4.5). The intimacy of the body in direct contact with its environment creates a more human-centered and experiential space that encourages participation. As Charles Eames noted about the design: "One is immediately drawn into

FIGURE 4.4 *George Nelson, Model Interior for Buckminster Fuller's Geodesic Dome, 1952. (© Vitra Design Museum, George Nelson Estate).*

thinking of the space as an experience. An experience in which one wants to take part ... it has little to do with conscious style and has a lot to do with human scale—and human need" (Eames 1957: 136–42). Function as well as psychological impact and human interaction are all considered in these 1950s designs. The model interiors of the Herman Miller catalogs, of Fuller's geodesic dome, and for the Experimental House all exude a sense of potential action, flexibility and delight-in-use that Nelson accentuates through his furniture designs, which are created in terms of multiple scenarios attainable through moving parts that facilitate a multitude of activities. The 1956 Herman Miller catalog highlights modular seating and storage units that can be configured in different ways to serve user's needs and space requirements. Nelson's bed design in the catalog includes a headboard that can be slanted at an angle to become a backrest for accommodating reading or eating in bed. As it slides down to become a backrest, it reveals bookshelves built in behind it to hold reading material. A radio folds out of the bottom half of the night stand between the beds if one prefers to listen to music. A lounge chair that is also featured includes a side table that clips onto either side. His design for a day bed includes the possibility of having back cushions that can be moved to any side. The coffee tables shown in the catalog contain components that pull out and serve as trays and the storage units are adjustable to accommodate a variety of sizes of objects. In the Nelson interior designs, as in the design of the traditional Japanese house, most functional and mechanical items are designed to fold away behind clean, undecorated surfaces until they are used. The lessons of the modularity, flexibility, and functionality of the Japanese house have all been incorporated in these designs, bringing with them the sense of flux, transition, and delight in the changes of daily life that are demonstrated in this traditional architecture. In contrast to the very artful yet complicated arrangements of the Eames house or the detached yet elegant strict formal arrangements of Mies's Tugendhat house, Nelson's interiors seem less stiff and more about being in them, than merely seeing them. His pillows, for example, are not strictly aligned like those in the Eames house, but have a sense of informality, potential for change, and the possibility of human occupation. They are scattered around in clusters like stones on a beach, less for visual impact and more to signify places where bodies might relax and be joined with these spaces. There is a sense of anticipation and life embodied in these as well as in the other objects of daily use, such as the open books, telephones, dishes, and ashtrays and details that are always depicted in Nelson's interiors (Figure 4.5).

Nelson presents users with spaces where, in Fromm's terms, one can attempt "to be" not merely just "have." In terms of being, they seem to embody an enhanced appreciation of space and the present tense that Nelson admired in the work of Frank Lloyd Wright: "The importance of Wright's

FIGURE 4.5 *George Nelson, Interior, Experimental House, 1951. (© Vitra Design Museum, George Nelson Estate).*

houses is not that they were in advance of their time ... the important thing is very simple: they enclose space as if it were precious, not for the sake of the space itself, but for the life that goes on within it"(Nelson 1946: 116–25). These interiors also capture the requisite surprise and delight that Yamasaki found in Japanese architecture. The intimate and human scales of the spaces, as well as the sense of discovery the users experience by figuring out how the flexible elements of the furniture work, create a direct connection between them and the physical world. This interaction in turn makes the users more aware of their environment and promotes an enhanced state of being. Whitehead characterizes this enhanced sense of being that comes through the initial apprehension of a situation as the "stage of Romance:" "The stage of romance is the stage of first apprehension. The subject matter has the vividness of novelty; it holds within itself unexplored connexions (sic) with possibilities half-disclosed by glimpses and half-concealed by the wealth of material" (Whitehead 1957: 17).

Nelson's manner of bringing this sense of being and delight to his interiors seems also to be accomplished by successfully translating the traditional Japanese design principles of wabi-sabi into contemporary materials and modern scenarios. Wabi and sabi are characteristics associated with Japanese aesthetics that have been defined and explored by a number of Western authors before Nelson. Both aesthetic categories are somewhat elusive and ephemeral. Writers analyzing them have identified them as difficult to explain but have also recognized that an understanding of them is crucial for understanding the distinct character of Japanese design. In The Book of Tea, Kakuzo Okakura, explains that wabi, which is literally translated as "poverty" "is a divestment of the material that surpasses material wealth. Wabi is simplicity that has shaken off the material in order to relate directly with nature and reality. This absence of dependence also frees itself from indulgence, ornateness, and pomposity. Wabi is quiet contentment with simple things" (Okakura 1989: 90). He further explains that wabi translated into the design of a tearoom results in the reduction of its components to the minimal necessary elements and to a visual field of simplicity and plainness. Material solidity and massiveness are avoided or are reduced as much as possible. This reduction creates a special "spatial awareness" and a sense of emptiness that is strangely exquisitely full. As Okakura adds, the fullness comes directly from its sense of incompleteness: "True beauty could only be discovered by one who mentally completed the incomplete. The virility of life and art lay in its possibility for growth" (Okakura 1989: 89). Daisetz Suzuki analyzes this concept in his treatise Zen and Japanese Culture: "Where you would ordinarily expect a line or a mass or a balancing element, you miss it, and yet this very thing awakens in you an unexpected feeling of pleasure" (Suzuki 1989: 24).

In Nelson's work of the 1950s one can recognize the principle of *wabi* first in the simplicity of forms and minimalist use of space and materials (Figure 4.3). There is a new exaggerated sense of leanness in his ensembles that enhances the aesthetic impact of the space surrounding them and incorporated by them. Materials and forms are pared down to their basic essentials but have not lost their "poetry." The spaces are rich in their emptiness. Like tea houses the proportions of the spaces are intimate and not massive. Writer/philosopher Leonard Koren explains in his book *Wabi-sabi for Artists, Designers, Poets and Philosophers:* "Things wabi-sabi are usually small and compact, quiet, and inward-oriented. They beckon: get close, touch, relate. They inspire a reduction of the psychic distance between one thing and another thing: between people and things" (Koren 1994: 67). The intimate scale and horizontality of the seating areas and furniture arrangements are countered by a sense of deep space behind them. The external limits of the ensembles are ambiguous, giving a sense of possible expansion and change. Nelson replicates here the special spatial awareness created by the characteristic of *wabi* that is exhibited in the design of traditional Japanese teahouse.

At the same time, the principle of *sabi* can also be seen at work in Nelson's pieces. *Sabi*, meaning literally "loneliness or solitude," refers to a sense of sadness or emotion. In Japanese culture, the concept of *sabi* most often is applied to objects that have a sense of history, use, imperfection, or crudeness—like wood left to weather in nature, a pattern made by water dripping too long on an object, or a utensil that shows the imprint of its use over time. In patinas acquired through age these objects convey a sense of sadness the same way a picture or memory may evoke a sense of poignancy. Objects with *sabi* are not shabby but bear the aesthetic impressions of wear and time that endow them with a sense of harmony, peace, and accentuated worth. Suzuki says "if an object suggests even superficially the feeling of an historical period, there is *sabi* in it" (Suzuki 1989: 24). Visually *sabi* translates into objects that are irregular, asymmetrical, and ambiguous. They are replete with a sense of flux, referring possibly the past as well the present condition.

Nelson's concern for respecting the nature of the materials and for allowing the individual textures, colors, and surfaces to stand for themselves yet work together to create a unified whole reflects an understanding of the principle of *sabi*. In his Rosewood cabinet series, for example, Nelson highlights the use of wood (Figure 4.6). Simple, flat planes of richly grained and colored Rosewood are used as doors to cabinets and as their focal points. The natural, unadorned wood allows the viewers/users to contemplate its natural organic quality and its past as living, growing tree. At the same time the strict geometric formal arrangements of his cabinet and its position on its slender metal-rod legs refer to its present condition as a particularly modern piece of furniture. A sense of the historical background of the organic material is successfully

5245 chest cabinet

FIGURE 4.6 *George Nelson, Rosewood Cabinet from Herman Miller Catalog, 1956. (© Vitra Design Museum, George Nelson Estate).*

combined with an understanding of the contemporariness that is a necessary part of its present place and function. Nelson's direct references to Japanese design types in his use of horizontal, and spare forms, shoji-like grids, and paper lantern-like lighting, references and enhance a sense of *sabi* in these designs, that is kept, however, within strictly defined limits since they are unmistakably part of the present in their reliance on such modern materials as plastics, metal, and plywood. Under Nelson's direction Japanese design is not merely copied or made into superficial knock-offs, but is translated into a purely modern idiom that clearly demonstrated a larger understanding of the workings of Japanese aesthetics. Nelson's borrowings from the Japanese enhances his design's characteristic naturalness, honesty, and delight that is so important to his version of modernism, while clearly creating a design that is representative of its own time and place. The simplicity, richness, and transcendence that he finds in the Japanese approach to aesthetics and incorporates in his work supports the directions encouraged by his mentors— to cast away mass-culture and the pursuit of possessions, to take Ortega's path of the "noble man," and to embrace Fromm's concept of being rather than having. Nelson noted his distain of the seemingly vacant world created by industrial capitalism and its emphasis on "things" that he was attempting to supplant in his work: "Like every one of my generation, I grew up in a social context which included a belief in progress so total that no one ever bothered to talk about it ... the key word [was] 'more,' more of everything, with the emphasis on the 'thing' in 'everything' .... A mass society [is a] strange, sleazy place" (Nelson, lecture 1987).

In Nelson's interiors of the 1950s, the feeling of pleasure, emotion, and satisfaction available to the users of his spaces is not a result of pride of possession or mere visual pleasure but comes from the enhancement of a sense of being through the processes of use. By means of its simplicity, elegance, truth-to-materials, honesty, and a sense of delight, Nelson's designs create a model of how less can indeed be more. This approach to design, not surprisingly, emulates the Zen practices embodied in some traditional Japanese designs that emphasize moment-by-moment awareness to promote a deeper understanding of the "nature of things" by direct experience. In both his writings and interiors, Nelson creates a type of Zen "koan,"[3] which attempts to project his users vividly into the present tense by subtle and complex means. As a designer and writer about design Nelson seems to take on a role similar to the Zen Master, an impression the designer Ettore Sottsass supports in his description of him: "I don't know if you have ever happened to receive a calm, absolutely calm man in your house, and suddenly to know that the air around you has changed, that words have changed, that all the normal reference points of your life have changed" (Abercrombie 2000: vi).

The influence of the Japanese, as well as his mentors, Fromm, Ortega, and Whitehead, lends Nelson's work in the 1950s the type of humanity that he believed modern design must have in order to be valid and useful for modern humankind. Because of it, Nelson's work exhibits a uniqueness, vitality, and vision that attempts to create an unselfconscious sense of comfort and enjoyment that Frederick Franck describes in *Zen and Zen Classics* as "what we have always been looking for without knowing it" (Franck 1978: 6). As a result Nelson was able to contribute significantly to the development of useful yet humane and beautiful interiors appropriate for modern life. As Sottsass again best summarizes: "George Nelson endeavored to design imaginary landscapes. He wanted to design for an American Society to come, a society that could have become the new society, invaded by prosperity, by certainties of technology, invaded by optimism—a relaxed society, a society capable of playing, a society capable of humour, and above all a society without fear" (Abercrombie 2000: ix).

5

The Interiors of Florence Knoll: Structure, Luxury, and the *Kunstwollen* of Postwar America

The elegance of Florence Knoll's[1] interior design, especially in projects such as the CBS headquarters she designed in 1952 (Figure 5.1), continues to be greatly admired and emulated as examples of classic modernism. Knoll was one of the first interior designers in the United States to specialize in commercial building projects in the post–Second World War period. As director and head designer of the Knoll Planning Unit, which was initiated in 1946, she developed her signature style known as the "Knoll Look,"[2] a stripped-down, but luxurious modern classicism, that became and still is the hallmark of high design in corporate America. As a woman designer, well known in her own right, not as a partner or member of an office under a man's direction, she plays an important role in modernism's history. Design historian R. Craig Miller notes: "Her interiors ... were the archetypes for corporate modernism of their time" (Miller 1983: 33). But she also can be seen as the archetype of what a women professional interior designer should be. Like many women making their way during the mid-century period, her story is one of continual self-improvement and education, the development of self-confidence and of having the ability to learn from her male mentors while establishing a unique identity apart from then. As with the previous designers considered, Florence Knoll's work was rooted in concept, feed by her education, experience, and interests and particularly the philosophical concerns and training of her mentors, Eliel Saarinen and Mies Van der Rohe whose influence helped her create her unique and distinguished way of creating modern interiors for American business.

FIGURE 5.1 *Florence Knoll, Office for Frank Stanton, CBS, 1952. (Florence Knoll Bassett Papers, American Archive of Art).*

Tragedy, training, and travel

Florence Schust Knoll was born in Michigan in 1917, the daughter of a wealthy family whose fortune was made in the baking industry. She was orphaned at age thirteen and placed under the care of a banker friend of the family, who arranged for her to attend the Kingswood School in Bloomfield Hills, Michigan. The Kingswood School was part of the arts and educational community, including the Cranbrook Academy of Art, that was developed by businessman George G. Booth and designed and implemented by Finnish designer Eliel Saarinen. At Kingswood, Knoll began to study design under the direction of Rachel de Wolfe Raseman, who was then the school's art director. In perhaps a therapeutic effort to soothe the homeless and parentless child, one of the first projects Raseman assigned Knoll was the design of a model home. Knoll worked enthusiastically on the assignment and produced a fully developed scale model of a two-story house with articulated interiors (Florence Knoll Bassett Papers, Box 1 Folder 1: 6). She also took classes with Eliel Saarinen and his wife Loja, who befriended the young girl and unofficially adopted her into their family. Knoll lived with the Saarinens during her years at Cranbrook and also traveled with them to Europe on their summer vacations.

By the time she graduated from Kingswood in 1934, Knoll had decided to become an architect. The Saarinens encouraged her to enroll in Cranbrook Academy before she applied to an accredited architectural school, so she studied there for about a year before moving to New York City in 1935 to attend the Columbia University School of Architecture's Town Planning program. She returned to Cranbrook the next year and began studying again with Eliel Saarinen. In the winter of 1937 she traveled to Italy with Cranbrook sculpture professor Carl Milles and his wife, enrolled in the University of Munich for a short time, and then joined the Saarinen family at their home in Finland and accompanied them on their yearly summer tour of Europe. On the advice of Alvar Aalto whom she met in Finland, she decided to attend the Architectural Association in London to complete her degree in the fall of 1938 (Makovsky 2001: 122). The outbreak of the Second World War, however, forced her to return to the United States in 1939 where she apprenticed with the newly transplanted Bauhauslers Walter Gropius and Marcel Breuer in Cambridge, Massachusetts, during the early part of 1940. In the fall of 1940 Knoll moved to Chicago to finally finish her architectural degree at the Illinois Institute of Technology under the direction of the master of modern architecture, Mies van der Rohe. After graduating from IIT in the spring of 1941, she moved to New York City to take a position with the architectural firm of Harrison and Abramowitz. This move brought her in contact with her future husband and business partner, Hans Knoll. Knoll, the son of a family that had established a successful furniture business in Germany, had recently moved to New York in 1938 to open his own venture, the Hans G. Knoll Furniture Company. He hired Florence Schust in 1943 to design interiors for his company and to initiate a new division of the company The Knoll Planning Unit. Hans Knoll soon realized that his new partner brought well-needed expertise to his operation. While he was the entrepreneur and salesperson, she had the talent and training to both choose and create designed products for the company. The couple was married in 1946 and together they formed the new company Knoll Associates, which would be the beginning of a corporate empire that would grow to eventually include fifteen showrooms and sales offices in the United States as well as licenses to sell furniture in twenty-four foreign countries. Their company not only supported the design and manufacture of modern furniture created by some of the most prominent designers of the day, such as Harry Bertoia, Marcel Breuer, Mies Van der Rohe, George Nakashima, and Jens Risom, but it also provided total interior design service through the Knoll Planning Unit, which Florence Knoll directed. The company later added a textile division that she also ran. Knoll Associates and its later expansion Knoll International provided one-stop shopping for all the goods and services needed to actualize modern interiors during the postwar period.

Florence and Hans Knoll shared an enthusiasm for modern design and worked together to bring Americans "superior designs, at low prices, by means of industrialization" (Izutsu 1992: 64). As the catalog for the *A Modern Consciousness* show at the Smithsonian in 1975, an exhibition about Florence Knoll's and D.J. dePree's work, points out, both she and her husband were ardent modernists: "Deeply committed to the cause of modern design, Florence and Hans Knoll crusaded for its acceptance in the same spirit, as one of their acquaintances has observed that 'the architects crusaded for modern architecture'" (Smithsonian 1975: 10). When Hans Knoll died unexpectedly in an automobile accident in 1955, Florence Knoll took over the directorship of the company and continued her design work. In 1959, after marrying banker/client Harry Hood Bassett, she sold her interest in Knoll Associates and retired from her position as president of the company the following year. She continued to work as a consultant and design director for the company until 1965 when she resigned after completing her final project, the CBS headquarters in New York, leaving a strong business and influential legacy still respected today.

Florence Knoll and European modernism

Florence Knoll, perhaps more than any other designer in this study, brings to the American interior design the legacy and philosophies of the early European modernists. The thread that connects her with these theories is well documented and begins with her relationship with the Saarinens and Cranbrook Academy. Soon after she arrived at the Kingswood School, both Eliel and Loja Saarinen took over the stewardship of Florence Knoll. She lived and traveled with the Saarinens and their two children, Eero and Pipsan, until she was married, was taught by them, and remained close friends with them all her life. Eliel Saarinen, a prominent architect in his native Finland at the turn of the century, first became known for his contributions to an emerging modern style influenced by Arts and Crafts, early modern, and traditional Finnish practices. His second-place prize for his design for the Chicago Tribune Tower competition in 1922 brought him worldwide attention and the money to travel to America in 1923 where he decided to settle. Saarinen's style of reduced, geometric, and abstracted forms appealed to wealthy businessman George G. Booth, whose son Henry had been a student of Saarinen's at the University of Michigan. Booth was interested in developing an educational community on his estate near Detroit and was impressed with Saarinen's total design approach. Booth and Saarinen embarked on a partnership that lasted from 1926 to 1943 and Saarinen and his family all became immersed in design and plans for the campus. Eliel Saarinen became president of Cranbrook Academy of Art in 1932.

His son, Eero Saarinen, graduated from Yale School of Architecture in 1934 and returned to Cranbrook to teach design and work in his father's practice. Although Yale at this time was still immersed in a Beaux Arts approach to design, his work with industrial designer Norman Bel Geddes in the early 1930s had given him an understanding of modern detailing and streamlining and his apprenticeship with Jarl Eklund in Helsinki a familiarity with the burgeoning International Style in Europe. The younger Saarinen returned to Cranbrook bringing new insights to both the school and his practice with his father. Eliel Saarinen, whose biographer Albert Christ-Janer noted, always embraced a philosophy of change, was open to learning from his son. Work by the father-son team, such as the First Christian Church in Columbus, Indiana, in 1939, show a marked reduction of form and new level of modern simplicity and abstraction. When Eero Saarinen went into practice for himself after the Second World War he became one of the premier modern architects of his time with distinguished projects ranging from the General Motors Technical Center (1948–56), to his design for Case Study Houses #8 and 9 with Charles Eames (1945–50), to his iconic TWA terminal in New York City (1956–62).

The Saarinens' home on the Cranbrook campus, whose design was contributed in part by all members of the family, provided Florence Knoll with a first-hand example of total design. Every feature of the home, from its structure to its smallest accouterment, was designed to work together to create an integrated and organic whole (Figure 5.2). The Saarinen family applied the same approach to their design for the Kingswood School where Knoll attended. This design lesson was supported by the family's ongoing discussions about design in both formal and informal venues. Florence could not have missed Eliel Saarinen and his family's lessons in total design, nor his personal view of what architecture meant to civilization as noted in his book *A Search for Form in Art and Architecture:*

> Architecture did not mean the building only: it meant the whole world of forms for man's protection and accommodation; it meant the various objects of the room as well as the room itself; it meant the building as such as well as the interrelation of buildings into organic groupings; and it meant the correlation of all the structural features into the complex organism of the city. (Saarinen 1948: 46)

This total design approach, which calls for the integration and interrelation of all elements of a design, would become an integral part of the philosophy, if not raison d'etre of Florence Knoll in her interiors for the Knoll Planning Unit.

FIGURE 5.2 *Saarinen House Living Room and Book Room, c. 1930. (Courtesy of Cranbrook Center for Collections and Research, Photo: James Haefner, 2015).*

Also echoed in her future work is the influence of her adopted brother Eero Saarinen, who worked closely with Knoll later on architectural projects and designs for the various furniture he created for the Knoll Company. The younger Saarinen not only reinforced his father's approach to total design, but also pushed further to integrate new technologies into modern forms appropriate for the new American lifestyle. Florence Knoll's translations of traditional office furniture into more contemporary technological materials such as steel, glass, plastic laminates and fiberglass in her furniture designs and its integration into the design of the interiors of the 1940s until the '60s, all share Eero Saarinen's same enthusiasms. Loja Saarinen, who was "talented in such things as interior design, photography and sculpture" and her daughter Pipsan, who with her created the numerous hand-woven textiles and carpets used in the Cranbrook projects, introduced her to a modern approach, vocabulary, and appreciation for textile design and interior furnishings (Izutsu 1992: 70). Knoll later credited Loja as the person who "stimulated [her] interest in texture and color" (Knoll Papers, Series 1, Box 1: 6), an interest that would continually demonstrate itself in the prominence that she gave to fine textiles and materials in her designs and for which she would become well known.

Florence Knoll's experience with prominent European modernists Gropius, Breuer, and Mies built on her education with the Saarinens and cemented her commitment to a European brand of modernism. Gropius and Breuer had only recently come to the United States via Britain from the Bauhaus in 1937 when she went to work for them as an unpaid apprentice in 1940. During Gropius and Breuer's short partnership that ended in 1941, they collaborated on the design of the Pennsylvania Pavilion for the 1939 New York World's Fair as well as design of several houses in the Boston area, including Gropius's own home. Knoll worked mostly on the residential designs, an experience that exposed her fully to the reduced geometric forms, asymmetrical massing, and vocabulary of industrial materials being used by these designers and can be seen in her own later designs. Both Gropius and Breuer taught at the newly restructured Harvard Graduate School of Design led by Joseph Hudnut, which played a significant role in integrating modern design into American architectural education. Both Gropius's and Breuer's belief in modern design, as well as their commitment to bringing its lessons to the United States, could not have been missed by their young apprentice.

The influence of Mies van der Rohe, however, is perhaps most evident in Knoll's work. The "Knoll Look," the aesthetic, which she is responsible for developing, epitomizes a Miesian classicism, and replicated his reduced forms, rational arrangements of spaces, and use of elegant materials, such as marble, polished chrome, leather and glass. Mies's approach to design was always situated in his overriding concern for structure. He posited, "Only where our purposes are realized in a meaningful structure can there be talk of architecture" (Blaser 1977: 23). This emphasis on the importance of structure is also clearly imprinted Florence Knoll's design approach. In an interview in 1982 she stated that she learned "greater clarification of design" from Mies and the importance of juxtaposition and detailing of materials and emphasized that "Mies taught me how to think and organize" (Miller 1983: 132).

The third thread that connects Florence Schust Knoll to European modernism is her relationship with Hans Knoll, who as a German was deeply influenced and inspired by the teachings of the Bauhaus. Author Akio Izutsu relates that "Hans liked and used the expressions 'the Bauhaus approach' and the 'the Bauhaus idea' in reference to his own work and own business" (Izutsu 1992: 64). More than any of Florence Knoll's mentors, Hans Knoll was particularly concerned with the integration of art and industry and using mass-production to provide its "superior designs, at low prices," "economy," "usefulness," "standardization," "flexibility," and "practicality," all Bauhaus ideals, which were buzzwords in the early Knoll advertising and promotions. A 1960 feature story on Knoll in the German publication *Der Spiegel* acknowledged the Bauhaus/ Knoll connection:

The development of products by the Knoll Company bears the fingerprints of the Bauhaus. The slogan at the Bauhaus was "new practicality, simple beauty, and functionality." The teaching staff and students at the Bauhaus were forced to emigrate to America following the school's closure, and whenever they constructed a new building there, it was the Knoll company that manufactured the furniture in accordance with their Bauhaus philosophy of new practicality, simple beauty, and functionality. (Izutsu 1992: 66)

Florence Knoll's relationship with former Bauhaus educators Gropius, Breuer, and Mies reinforced her husband's admiration and emulation of the school's philosophies and ideals. After her husband died in 1955, she continued his quest to bring the Bauhaus ideal to the American setting and brought into full-scale production Bauhaus designs, such as the now-classic Wassily and Cesca chairs designed by Breuer as well as such Mies-designed International Style furniture as his Barcelona and MR chairs.

Common philosophies, common issues

While the designs of the Knoll Company are often characterized as related to the aesthetics of the Bauhaus School—through general association as well as the company's own promotion material—Florence Knoll's personal approach to design, which is reflected ultimately in the "Knoll Look," is more directly influenced by Eliel Saarinen and Mies van der Rohe. As Knoll biographer Bobbye Tigerman explains:

> Knoll's accomplishments are due to her natural design talent, positioning in an environment that exposed her to progressive currents in the architectural and design worlds, and proximity to some of the most prominent architects and designers of the day. She never claimed nor exhibited forceful independence from the influences around her. Rather she wove together the lessons learned from a variety of mentors to produce her distinctive style. (Tigerman 2005: 20)

Although they each produced two very distinct kinds of designs, Saarinen and Mies shared a number of important assumptions about design, including the importance of structure and form, a concern for aesthetics as well as function, and a belief that appropriate design needed to reflect the spirit of the times. These commonalities are their legacy to Florence Knoll, whose interiors bear both their imprints. Although Saarinen and Mies appear to be a generation apart from their architectural styles, the former being most associated with

Arts and Crafts, while the latter seemingly epitomized the International Style, they were only thirteen years apart in age. Both were born in the nineteenth century (Saarinen b.1873 and Mies b.1886) and came to their professions during a time that was fully considering the implications of a modern society. As such, both of their personal and formalized educations were greatly influenced by emerging modern considerations of both art and design.

Eliel Saarinen first trained as a painter. He was a frequent visitor to the art collection at the Hermitage in St. Petersburg, and when he graduated from the Polytekniska Institutet in Helsingfors, Finland in 1897, he was awarded a scholarship to travel in Europe. From his travels, which became a yearly event (that Florence Knoll later participated in), he became familiar with new developments in the arts and met and developed friendships with proponents of modernism, such as Alvar Aalto, Peter Behrens, Gustav Mahler, and Josef Olbrich. A major influence on Saarinen's education was his friendship with the art critic Julius Meier-Graefe, who became a frequent visitor at the Saarinen estate, Hvitträsk, and resided there while working on his monograph on the artist Paul Cézanne. Saarinen's integrated approach to design, his attention to function combined with aesthetics, and his celebration of appropriate materials reflect Meier-Graefe's understanding of the idea of *Gesamtkunstwerk* (total work of art) as well as his concept of "moralischen Luxus." As Meier-Graefe scholar Kenworth Moffet explains: "By 'Luxus' he [Meier-Graefe] meant the beautiful and sensuous effects; by 'moralisch[en],' of course he meant the integrity of function. The new art was to eschew historicism yet retain the richness of the eye, intimacy of spirit, and bright colorfulness that would satisfy sensibilities nurtured by Impressionist paintings" (Moffett 1973: 31). Saarinen's designs, which always integrate exterior, interior, furniture, and details in a unified whole (as in the buildings he designed for the Cranbrook campus), also incorporate an honest and rich use of materials that enhances both the physical and emotional function of the space. Saarinen's own fully developed philosophy, which supports this approach to design, was outlined in detail in his 1948 publication *A Search for Form: A Fundamental Approach to Art*, a personal treatise in which Saarinen attempted to justify and inspire the need for each new generation to create new modes of artistic expression that were appropriate for their time. His arguments center around a discussion of form, which he views as the essential quality of art and design and he elaborates in detail how concepts such as "truth," "beauty," "logic," "function," and "imagination" relate to it. The book was meant to be not only a historical overview of how these concepts have played out throughout art history, but a practical guide to the creative process for contemporary artists and designers.

Mies van der Rohe was also directly immersed in theoretical discussions regarding an emergent modernism. He began his education in the building trades, working not only with his father, who was a stonemason, but attending the trade school in his home town of Aachen in Germany from 1900 to 1902. He later apprenticed with furniture-maker Bruno Paul from 1905 to 1907 and architect and interior design Peter Behrens from 1908 to 1911. Behrens had been one of the founding members of the Munich Secession and of the United Workshop for Craftsmanship and before he became director of the Arts and Crafts College in Düsseldorf in 1903 he worked at the Darmstadt Artist's Colony. Paul was also a founding member of the United Workshop for Craftsmanship. These involvements brought both of them to the forefront of the German Arts and Crafts movement and its efforts to reconcile art with new industrial practices. Both Paul and Behrens were responsible for production lines of machine-produced furniture for the United Workshop from 1908 to 1912 that were promoted as "standard furniture," appropriate for "the working man"(Gössel, Leuthäuser, and Sembach 1991: 77). Projects such as Behrens's well-publicized model dining room created for an exhibition at the Dresden Workshop in 1903 exhibited a modern approach that emphasized the truth to materials and reduced geometric form that both Behrens and Paul used to create elegant, useful spaces that were appropriate for their time period. Mies's first training in design with these men would have introduced him to this approach. This experience would have been augmented by his lifelong love of learning and reading. Phyllis Lambert, a Mies scholar writes that "Mies read avidly in the sciences and philosophy from age nineteen until his death in 1969 at the age of eight-three" (Lambert 2001: 193). At the time of his death his private library held over 800 volumes. From his documented writings and discussions that centered around his association with Behrens, the Deutscher Werkbund, the Arbeitsrat für Kunst (Working Council for Art), the Weissenhof model housing exhibition, the Bauhaus, and avant-garde publications such as *Frühlicht, G2, Die Form,* it is clear that Mies was totally immersed in contemporary considerations of modern design and theory. Architectural historian Werner Oechslin points out that Mies's mentor, Peter Behrens, was at the forefront of discussions concerning the link between architectural creation and the use of technology. A particular concern of Behrens in this discussion was the notion of style. Oechslin notes that Behrens considered the ideas of Alois Riegl, Gottfried Semper, and Heinrich Wölfflin in his writings and work and that "Mies followed the discussion at close range" (Lambert 2001: 27–30). Behrens concluded that stylistic classifications, such as Wofflin's Baroque "massiveness" are not, as Semper theorized, derived from function or technology but from what Riegl referred to as *Kunstwollen* or "artistic will" (Lambert 2001: 25–30). Critic Arthur Danto briefly but aptly summarizes this major theory of Alois Riegl: "Riegl never went into any depth on what exactly constituted the *Kunstwollen*, but his use of the term allowed him to consider the history of art of a given period as exhibiting a kind of internal drive or purpose, which realized itself progressively through time"

(Arthur Danto 2000: 2). Behrens embraced this idea in his own theoretical approach to design. "We understand style as the unified formal expression resulting from the collective manifestations of spirit of a given epoch," he stated in 1913 at the *Kongress für Ästhetik und Allgemeine Kunstwissenschaft* held in Berlin (Lampert 2001: 27). Both Mies van der Rohe and Eliel Saarinen seem to embrace the concept of *Kunstwollen* (perhaps inspired in this direction from their mutual study and admiration of the work of Behrens) and came to other similar conclusions about the appropriate nature of modern design that eventually would influence the work of their student Florence Knoll. Mies was more specific about the appropriateness of the concept of *Kunstwollen* in regard to the field of design, when he defined architecture as "neither theory nor aesthetic speculation nor doctrine but the spatially apprehended will of the epoch. Alive, changing, new" (Neumeyer 1991: 241). Werner Blaser, a Mies scholar, elaborates on his perspective:

> Mies van der Rohe believes that architecture is not bound to the day, not to eternity, but to the epoch ... Architecture is the interpretation of a happening in history, the genuine consummation of its inner movement, the fulfillment and expression of its essential nature ... to express the significant driving forces of our era. (Blaser 1994: 11)

In *The Search for Form*, Eliel Saarinen also integrated *Kunstwollen* as part of his personal philosophy of design. In his attempt to define the concept of style in relation to art and design he theorized that "style means a sequential process of spontaneous yet conducive actions that spring from the physical and spiritual characteristics of the time and people" (Saarinen: 186). Much of Saarinen's discussion in *The Search for Form* revolves around his central concept of "fundamental form." Saarinen links the concept of fundamental form with that of *Kunstwollen* when he describes it as the stylistic embodiment of the "fundamental characteristics of the time." "Fundamental form" is not a fixed concept but is a "constant, sequent, and forward-moving achievement of the creative instinct," he posits. "[It] is not an intentional achievement of man. It grows determinatively from the soul of the age. It is the agency which directs man's work during that age" (Neumeyer 1991: 163). As Saarinen foregrounds in his writing, the "search for form" is the primary impetus that drives the development of an essential form for the modern epoch. For Saarinen, this search for form implied an honest and sincere attempt to understand one's world better. The study of the intimate workings and constructions of nature, for example, could offer models for appropriate forms for art and design. The study of the nature of materials, whether natural or man-made, also pointed the designer to appropriate formal considerations for architecture and design, As Saarinen stated in an interview in *Pencil Points* magazine: "The only thing we are sure of—a thing we must always keep in mind—is that we should begin with simple forms, looking for truth and logic in regard both to construction and to materials" (Saarinen 1929: 202).

For Mies the "logic and truth" of construction and materials, as well as the design as a whole, was the embodied in the term he called "structure." Mies's concept of structure, like Saarinen's concept of form, is related to *Kunstwollen*. "True architecture is always objective and is the expression of the inner structure of our time, from which it stems," he stated (Blaser 1994: 6). Like Saarinen, Mies believed that the pursuit of an understanding of structure was the key not only to understanding the *Kunstwollen* of the period, but also to creating appropriate, meaningful, and substantive design. For both Mies and Saarinen, designs derived from a rational approach concerned primarily with form and structure was the most appropriate for the modern epoch and the material and aesthetic manifestation of its *Kunstwollen*. For both, *Kunstwollen* was a generating force that was reflected in design of all levels from the macrocosm of the city plan to the microcosm of furniture and interior accessories.

For Saarinen the rational approach to design he saw as appropriate for the modern epoch is formally reflected in all his designs, from cities to furniture, through his consistent inclusion of a linear axis against which the ordered balance of asymmetrical arrangements of thrusting vertical forces and contrasting and grounding horizontal volumes could be anchored. As early as his design for the Molchow-Haus in Brandenburg in 1905, he was noted for his use of clean, simple lines that hold the textures and material together in a harmonious arrangement. Albert Christ-Janer, Saarinen's biographer, commented on the project and of its appropriateness for contemporary interior design:

> Of particular interest to the student of contemporary design, however, is the clean, unhampered line of the interior. There, skillfully combined, are the quietly refined rooms, with light and generous space enriched by a thoughtful array of textures, and the simple furniture created to harmonize with the whole .... [the] clean, thin quality was transferred with logic into the nature of the interior and furniture. (Christ-Janer 1948: 28)

Mies, as well, was noted for his use of a rational grid as a unifying force in his so-called "skin and bones" structures. Mies characterized his design strategy in the following statement: "The unswerving determination to dispense with all accessories and to make only what is essential the object of the creative work, the determination to confine oneself to clear structure alone is not a limitation but a great help." As Blaser elaborates: "Structure in these terms is a constructed system of relations, a constructive form rationally thought out in all its details" (Blaser 1994: 11). This inter-relational and systematic approach to structure, that is not only a hallmark of Mies's work but of a new generation of design, is elegantly played out in such early projects as the Barcelona Pavilion of 1929, in which he contains and controls both plan and section in a dynamic and expanding orthogonal grid. In this design, a rationally controlled arrangement of lines and planes holds together a sensuous palette of rich materials, such as marble, chrome and wood. This approach is extended out to the site by means of the transparent expanses of glass in the window walls, and the arrangement of furniture and artwork on the patio beyond the enclosed interior spaces. Exterior, interior, furniture, and detail are all unified together within this overarching "constructive form."

At the same time, although the overall aesthetic impact of both Saarinen's and Mies's work is controlled by rational systems, it is never merely functional. Both designers rejected a purely functional approach and never denied both the symbolic and sensuous qualities of both their forms and materials in their search for appropriate modern design. "Why should the form of our age necessarily be meaninglessly reproductive or mechanically dry?" Saarinen asked in *A Search for Form* (Saarinen 1948: 309). His son, Eero, bluntly summed up his father's opinion the best: "Strict functionalism was a necessary purgative, but after all, there is nothing aesthetic about an enema" (Saarinen 1956: 57). Likewise Mies, while identifying form as a primary generator of his designs, eschewed both pure formalism and pure functionalism. "Form as a goal is formalism; and that we reject" (Neumeyer 1991: 242), he stated. His student John Barney Rogers encapsulated Mies's philosophy on this topic when he stated in a lecture: "Construction has no meaning until handled with aesthetic intent" (Rogers 1935: 4–5). A concern for aesthetics, beauty, and meaning is foregrounded in both Saarinen's and Mies's designs through their use of materials. In Saarinen's interiors at Cranbrook Academy, such as the living room of the Saarinen Home (Figure 5.2), a strict orthogonal arrangement of parts controls and connects the overall plan, while warm natural wood surfaces are juxtaposed with custom-designed tapestries, draperies, and rugs of linen and wool in a subdued but rich palettes of vermillion, silver, and gray (by Loja and Pipsan Saarinen) and aluminum lighting fixtures, which all contribute to a simple, well-ordered, yet sumptuous setting. In Mies's Barcelona Pavilion materials equally take the forefront. Its gleaming chrome columns and use of accentuated patterns of travertine, marble, and onyx, green opalescent glass, and rich leathers bring to the modern interior a sense of luxuriousness, which came to be highly admired but is often missing in much of early modern design. Mies, like Saarinen, seems to embrace Meier-Graefe's concept of "moralischen Luxus." In his designs, a rational overlay, characterized by reduction of form, orthogonal geometry, and mathematical precision (moralisch), is used to control and contain a sensuous selection of rich materials (Luxus). By means of this strategy, in both Saarinen's and Mies's designs, the binary oppositions of rational/expressive, architecture/decoration, physical/psychological, body/mind, and masculine/feminine are held in balance, and work in combination to enhance yet control each other. By doing so both designers are able to translate successfully the status, aesthetics and sensuousness associated with fine materials that one finds in historical designs (such as the Palace at Versailles, for example) into an acceptable modern idiom. Rational structure and luxury are successfully bonded in both men's interiors into an aesthetic that is unmistakably of and for its time period. This aspect of their designs proved to be particularly appealing to the new corporate businessman of the post–Second World War period, who wished to display with discretion the badges of their success while appearing progressive and modern. The lessons learned by Florence Knoll from both Saarinen and Mies in this regard form the basis for her postwar designs.

The Knoll Look

Florence Knoll's prominence and success were based in the interior design work she did for the Knoll Planning Unit. Both Hans and Florence Knoll had noticed the need not only for modern products, but an approach to design that was able to incorporate them. She summed up the problem in 1964 in her article on interior design for the *Encyclopedia Britannica*:

> Prior to World War II most nonresidential interiors were either designed by the architects for the buildings or were not designed at all. More often than not, the building itself was at violent odds with its interior requirements; The reason these architects had to design their own interiors down to lighting fixtures and doorknobs was obvious: the "interior decorators" of the time had no knowledge of modern architecture—or, if they had, they were generally out of sympathy with it. (Izutsu 1992: 84)

The Knoll Planning Unit was created in 1946 to sell professional interior design services to a specifically contract market (office, schools, industry) and to provide both the expertise and products needed to create specifically modern interiors. The furniture produced and sold by Knoll was never considered in terms of individual products but as components that are integral parts of larger designs and essential elements in the construction of space. The success of the Knoll Planning Unit was based in selling this concept of total design to the public and particularly to corporate America. Florence Knoll's totally integrated approach to design for the interior environment became known as the "Knoll Look." This look distilled European modernism and the particular lessons learned from her mentors, Eliel Saarinen and Mies van der Rohe into an appropriate American genre for the post–Second World War corporate America. The success of the Knoll Look and The Planning Unit propelled the Knoll Company into prominence in the 1940s and '50s through its highly publicized interior designs for companies such as Connecticut General Insurance (1954–57), Columbia Broadcasting System (1952 and 1965), and H.J. Heinz (1958).

The Knoll Look incorporated well-designed modern objects, such as furniture designed by Knoll, Mies, Eero Saarinen, and Harry Bertoia, into a simple, ultimately functional, and yet extremely elegant visual field. Like Mies and Saarinen, Florence Knoll's approach was a rational one that considered functional needs as the generator but not the dictator of the design aesthetic. The Knoll Planning Unit utilized a five-step design process that fully analyzed the work function and conditions of their business clients to develop a total design that was efficient, highly usable, and extremely aesthetic. "Space planning," which is a European modernist concept first developed by Adolf Loos in his *raum plan* (space plan), was incorporated in this process and used as a primary focus around which, as in the designs of Mies and Saarinen, all the other details of the space—furniture choice and placement, kinds of materials, location of lighting and mechanical equipment, etc.—revolved. Florence Knoll's particular approach to space planning was based on a concern for structure and organized space, classically modern furniture, a range of materials, as well as a consideration of mechanical requirements within strictly orthogonal arrangements that held most all of the components of the design securely in a parallel and perpendicular three-dimensional grid (Figure 5.3). By overlaying this rational structure on to the plan of her designs, Florence Knoll not only created the most efficient layout of space, but also significantly altered the paradigm for corporate office planning. As Bobbye Tigerman explains in her analysis of Knoll's office planning: "Traditionally desks were oriented in a corner of the office on a diagonal. But beginning with Nelson Rockefeller's 1946 office, the Planning Unit placed the desk perpendicular to the wall to conserve space. Hans Knoll's 1951 office at the New York Headquarters of Knoll Associates popularized this move" (Tigerman 2005: 53). Florence Knoll elaborated on this shift: "The parallel or L-shaped plan made sense, and it saved square footage. This convinced our corporate clients who were satisfied to move from the diagonal plan with a solid desk in front and a table behind" (Florence Knoll Basset Papers, Series 1: 21). Beyond being efficient and functional, the parallel and perpendicular arrangement of Knoll's designs also placed the furniture and components of the interior design under the controlling order of the architectural envelope, creating a

FIGURE 5.3 *Florence Knoll, Deering Milliken Salesroom, New York City, 1948. (Florence Knoll Bassett Papers, American Archive of Art).*

fusion of architectural space and its contents. By this method, the rationality or "structure" of the building was extended into every detail and fixture of the interior.

Knoll's reliance on this defining structure follows the lessons of both Saarinen and Mies, who also employed the grid of the architecture as the controlling mechanism for their interior components. This rational structural approach to space planning branded Knoll's interiors as appropriately modern. "Since its inception the Knoll organization has endeavored to design and produce furnishings and interiors appropriate to contemporary architecture and suited to the changing needs of modern living," Knoll stated (Knoll Associates, Inc. 1961: 3). But at the same time this approach linked the designs also to the inherent rationality of modern corporate America and its calls for orderly, organized, functional, efficient, and effective processes. As design historian Alexandra Lange points out: "The mid-century architect working for a major industry had to adapt their [sic] practice to a different scale and structure … [and] embrace of the dominant corporate concerns for repeatability, expansion and economics of scale, as well as the sense of technological adventure that fueled corporate growth after Second World War" (Lange 2006: 236). Tigerman supports this assertion specifically in respect to Florence Knoll's designs: "The Knoll Look constituted a code or language of signs that communicated corporate modern design … This corporate modernism drew on the associations of the modern period with progress and efficiency while acknowledging the need for a humanized interior environment" (Tigerman 2005: 57). Florence Knoll's designs therefore can be seen as a visual expression of the modern corporate ethos and the *Kunstwollen* of modern design of this time period.

One of the first examples of Florence Knoll's approach to interior design and the emerging Knoll Look, which would be later be promulgated by the Knoll Planning Unit, was the design for her husband's office in 1949 (Figure 5.4).

FIGURE 5.4 *Florence Knoll, Office for Hans Knoll, 1949. (Florence Knoll Bassett Papers, Archives of American Art).*

In this fifteen-foot by fifteen-foot space Knoll created the prototype for the modern executive office. In this design, all furniture and accessories are held in place by a parallel and perpendicular grid that acknowledges the architectural envelope while at the same time making the most economical use of the space. Knoll lowered the ceiling height, which not only increased the sense of horizontal space in the room, but also lowered the center point of the back wall, bringing it closer to eye level. This change literally centered the focus of the room on her husband's head as he sat at his desk, and thus stressed his importance in the space. The status of his position is mutually constructed and reflected by the rational predictability of the design. This effect was augmented by painting a black accent wall behind the desk, which created a sense of deep space as well as a backdrop for focusing on him. The storage cabinets around the room were low in profile so as not to detract from this directed view and built in not only to economize space, but to also put them under the control of the architectural grid. The freestanding desk echoed the minimal articulations of the room by being a simple, unadorned slab wood top that was suspended in space by elegant square chrome metal legs, which allowed the space to flow unimpeded underneath it. Simple side and desk chairs, also with metal legs, reinforced the spatial arrangements of the plan without crowding it. For Knoll the simple square-sectioned metal frames that she used on most her furniture and portable wall partitions translate the architectural steel framing of the modern building into the smaller scale of the individual interior spaces and provided the "moralisch" component of Meier-Graefe's "moralischen Luxus."

The "Luxus" component, however, is equally expressed through Knoll's elegant use of expressive and sensuous materials, which indicate the sense of status and luxury that was also a necessary part of corporate America's view of itself. Like Mies and Saarinen, Florence Knoll understood this need and embraced the use of materials to physically, aesthetically, and symbolically enhance her designs. The simplicity of detail of Hans Knoll's office was made rich and even opulent through the use of materials like the wheat-colored Indian silk for the floor-to ceiling curtains and the teak top of the desk. Perhaps, because of her earlier experience at Cranbrook and work with textiles designers like Loja Saarinen and Marianne Strengell, textiles were a particularly essential element of her interior environments. She opened a textile division in 1947 so that the company could produce fabrics specifically for their furniture and interiors and throughout her career she traveled around the world researching textile design and construction (Izutsu 1992: 70). Both the importance and the total integration of the various materials, particularly the textiles, into an overall design scheme was highlighted by Florence Knoll's method of making drawings that included gluing swatches of materials directly onto them (Figure 5.5). This collage

FIGURE 5.5 *Florence Knoll, "Paste-Up" for Office of Hans Knoll, 1949. (Florence Knoll Bassett Papers, American Archive of Art).*

method of presentation, as noted by numerous authors, was a favorite of fashion designers and was used by Loja Saarinen in a pasted mock-up she made of an evening dress she was designing as a gift for Knoll. This collage format, however, was also a favored means of presentation used by Mies van der Rohe, who was perhaps influenced by the work of Kurt Schwitters and Georges Braque whose art he collected. Mies often overlaid his architectural drawings with collaged elements that indicated stone, brick, wood, color, and artwork. For Loja Saarinen, Mies, and Florence Knoll, the inclusion of these collaged elements, referring to the materials and details of their designs was a way of acknowledging their importance to the designers and this practice added a sense of physicality, sensuality, and life to their design proposal. The "paste-up," as it was called by the Planning Unit, was an important part of Florence Knoll's approach to conceptualizing interiors that is still replicated today by many interior designers and became a personal trademark of her work. As Florence Knoll pointed out: "It was extraordinary how small swatches of fabric and wood could convey a feeling of space … I always felt the need to employ this system that eventually was used by design offices as a standard" (Florence Knoll Bassett Papers, Series 5, Folder 20).

The design for Hans Knoll's office can be seen as one of the first manifestations of the Knoll Look, which was further developed and promoted by Florence Knoll and the Planning Unit in their designs for the Knoll Showrooms (Figure 5.6). The Knoll Showrooms served two main purposes. The first was to house and display various design products produced and sold by the Knoll Company. Knoll Associates had taken the lead in the 1940s in manufacturing and promoting products designed by a large variety of prominent and emerging contemporary designers from all around the world. They were the first to manufacture the classic designs first developed in Europe by Mies van der Rohe and Marcel Breuer, such as the "Barcelona," "Wassily," and "Cesca" chairs, and make them accessible to general public. The famous Hardoy "Butterfly Chair" and Saarinen's "Womb" chair were also Knoll products. Designs by Franco Albini, Hans Bellman, Harry Bertoia, George Nakashima, Ralph Rapson, and Jens Risom were all produced by Knoll. Instead of visiting a showroom and seeing the work of only one or two designers (George Nelson and Ray and Charles Eames, for example, designed most of the products sold by the Herman Miller Furniture Company), one could visit Knoll Associates and

FIGURE 5.6 *Florence Knoll, Interior of Knoll Showroom, San Francisco, 1957. (Florence Knoll Bassett Papers, Archives of America).*

find a wide assortment of designs from all over the world. In this endeavor, the Knoll Company perhaps best expresses the Bauhaus ideas that Hans Knoll brought to the company, including realizing the school's goals of integrating art and industry as well as making good design available to the general public through mass production.

The second purpose of the showrooms was to market the concept of modern interior design and promote the services provided by the Knoll Planning Unit as necessary ones. The showrooms, which were mostly housed in old townhouses, in the early years, provided Knoll with an excellent opportunity to demonstrate how traditional architectural spaces could be transformed into modern space. In 1948 Florence Knoll re-designed the company's New York City showroom, which *Architectural Record* described as "spacious but intimate; simple but subtle". R. Craig Miller posits, "It was the New York showroom [1951, which was located in an open loft space] that marked a dramatic change in Florence Knoll's work and the beginning of the 'Knoll Look'" (Miller 1983: 140). In the design for this showroom Knoll introduced a structural system of black steel channels holding suspended color panels, which were used as walls and ceilings. In doing so, she demonstrates how both a new structural system and a new architectural envelope could be inserted into a historical building. Various components of the interior, including furniture, built-in storage, artwork, and mechanical systems were then designed to work in conjunction within this new structural system. Against a mostly white background Knoll juxtaposed primary colors to establish a system of coordinating and establishing discrete areas and reinforcing hierarchies. This strategy was repeated often in her work, and was used in the design of the CBS offices in order to differentiate separate spaces in the large overall open-office plans.

The showroom displays were also case studies in how to incorporate status and symbolism into a design by means of furniture and materials. Industrial products such as fiberglass, metal, and birch wood were often used to designate a lower or middle-level office work space, while richer materials like marble, thick glass, teak, and rosewood, as well as wool carpets indicated areas of higher status. Throughout the space, however, the formal qualities of the design, the regulating grid, and the general design characteristics of the furniture and accessories remained the same and lent the overall design a strong sense of harmony. Other design firms emulated this successful combination of unity and variety as well as the use of materials to establish hierarchy. Miller notes that "by the mid-fifties, Knoll had become an international operation; Florence Knoll's showrooms had made modern American design truly an 'international style.' At home, the 'Knoll Look' became an accepted standard for American corporations through a series of executive offices designed by Knoll and the Planning Unit" (Miller 1983: 142). In these showroom designs, Florence Knoll established a new vocabulary that would be used to express individual status, a company's success, and the American corporate office's overall commitment to modernity, which was viewed in terms of progress. As Virginia Lee Warren described in her review of Florence Knoll's career in the *New York Times* in 1964:

> Once upon a time virtually every big business executive thought ... that his office had to have pale green walls and that his heavy, drawers-to-the-floor desk had to be placed cater-cornered. Then along came a woman who showed the executive that they could be just as impressive against a background of neutral or even white walls sometimes with one wall in a strong primary color, and that their status would not be impaired if they moved their desks to a logical, space-saving four square position. (Warren 1964: 40)

This transformation of the American corporate office as expressed through the Knoll Look is perhaps best embodied in Florence Knoll's last project, the interiors for the CBS corporate headquarters offices in New York in 1965. Knoll returned briefly from her retirement from the Knoll Planning Unit to complete the interiors for this building that was designed by her lifelong friend Eero Saarinen, who had died of a brain tumor before the project could be completed. This building, as all Saarinen's projects, reflected his commitment to the idea of the total design. As Izutsu recounts in his overview of the project: "Saarinen believed that the architect had to take the responsibility not only for landscaping and furniture, but for everything else as well, right down to the ashtrays" (Izutsu 1992: 89).

The CBS building was designed on a five-foot module, which Knoll used as the basis of her space planning and design of its 35 floors and 868 individual rooms. Mechanical equipment such as phones, televisions, and record players were built into the architecture and furniture to unify the functional features of the space and minimize their visual impact on the overall aesthetic of the spaces. Fiberglass, plastics, metal, and varying accent walls of high-chroma colors designated lower hierarchy work spaces and helped designate different kinds of spaces, while linen curtains, bronze velvet wall coverings, French walnut paneling, Tiffany glass, a bronze desk with an marble top, and a Mies Brno chair were used to indicate the high status of company president Frank Stanton's executive suite and to create what R. Craig Miller describes as "the most sumptuous executive offices in America of their time" and "no greater swansong" for the retired designer (Miller 1983: 142).

Like Saarinen and Mies, Florence Knoll successfully combined a rational approach to design with the use of rich and varied materials to create an appropriate interior design not only for successful American businesses but also for her time. Functionality, durability, usefulness, and economy of means are expressed in a style that leaves room for the symbolic indicators of personal expression and corporate wealth and power. In doing so, she created a particularly appealing and appropriate kind of design for the American business. As Miller concludes:

> Her work shows that she learned the lessons of industrial design from the Bauhaus, a purity and elegance from Mies, and the concept of total design from Eliel Saarinen. The resultant style—the "Knoll Look"—was so pervasive that it came to symbolize American interior design in the 1950s and sixties. It was a singular union: a design of objects and interiors of international renown and a principal of one of the most influential design firms of her time. No American designer since Louis Comfort Tiffany could claim such a mantle. (Miller 1983: 143)

Like her mentors, Knoll was able to recognize and embody the concerns of her era into her designs. Embedded in these are key issues of her age and its *Kunstwollen* which can be read in the design, Alexandra Lange so aptly points out as, "changes in postwar American architecture culture, changes which expanded the role of the architect in both corporate and civic life" (Lange 2006: 234). Using her signature style, the Knoll Look, which integrated her education and experience into a stunning demonstration of the teachings of her mentors and of the principles of *moralischen Luxus* Florence Knoll not only lent creditability to the new field of interior design by making it an important part of American business practice, but also demonstrated how powerful interior design could be as a means to present and promote the progressive and successful character of corporate America.

Conclusion

During the mid-century modern period, interior design emerged as a professional and academic discipline that as Edgar Kaufmann jr. succinctly noted was based in "principles not effects." Unlike today when preconceived ideas frame both its use and audience, interior design in these years was flexible, expansive, and not yet rigidly defined. This allowed proponents from various backgrounds and trainings to practice it in a variety of ways and a broad range of questions to be considered. For the Eameses, interior design was a vehicle to communicate their interest and investigation of the power of the visual field through a living demonstration of it. For George Nelson, it was the medium of an intellectual and thinker who wished to incorporate philosophical concerns into design in order to create a more humane world. For Russel and Mary Wright, the domestic interior was the place to express and promote a specifically American character. For Richard Neutra, it was a laboratory in which to explore the relation of health and built space. And for Florence Knoll, the interior was a symbolic yet functional expression of the energy of the contemporary workplace and the means to connote success and prosperity in an appropriate modern form. As design historian Penny Sparke has aptly pointed out, the interior "unlike … graphic or fashion design, … is constantly in flux and, to make it even more of a moving target, is composed of a multitude of variables both material and immaterial" (Sparke and McKellar eds. 2004: 2). This flexible character of interior design made it especially useful as an investigative medium to these early practitioners of mid-century modern. The designers considered here all recognized the potential of the interior as a means not only to ask and answer questions but to share those answers with a larger audience and impact the way lives were lived.

For the most part, the study of interior design deals primarily with imagined rather than actual spaces. When creating an interior design, the designer visualizes an ideal space, which is depicted in drawings and models and then elaborated in a finished and pristine end product that is as yet unused and unmodified by occupation. Documentations of interior designs are presentations of this ideal state at the completion of a project—the end point of the designer's involvement. Design magazines and history books most often never show the project after it has been inhabited or how it might change over time. Although some contemporary magazines are beginning to show interiors in and after use and designers like Eames documented their house as they lived in it, the documentation of mid-century modern is usually the static depiction of the interior as imagined by the designer, completed, and in an ideal state staged for photography. This book has not concerned itself, therefore, with the question of the effectiveness of the real spaces, many of which are not still in existence, as compared to the ideas that might have inspired them conceptually. It would be difficult to prove now whether Knoll's designs for the CBS corporate offices really did make it a more efficient place to work, or if George Nelson's interiors were really humane, or if Neutra's interiors made someone a healthier and better person. While these questions could possibly be proved or disproved, and to a certain extent have been speculated on, it is significant to note that it was not this book's goal to ascertain those claims. What was most important was attempting to discern and understand the design's inspiration and intent—its "principles" not its "effects."

The principles at work in the interiors considered here were diverse and drawn from a variety of sources, influences, and ideas, shaped by their designers' experience and interests. And although it seems clear that mid-century modern interior design in America does not stem from one consistent and shared set of principles, there are commonalities to these designers' intents. First, to be modern and representative of their time. Second, to enhance humankind through the design of the environment. And third, to explore and promulgate specific principles and ideas to a larger public through the medium of the interior. The seriousness of these shared intents, in addition to the philosophical and theoretical concepts that influenced each designer's projects differently, lends them all a sense of gravity, richness, and higher purpose that is not always visible in contemporary interior design. In his final chapter of his biography of George Nelson, Stanley Abercrombie remarked: "New chair designs [today] satisfy and also partly provoke a restless search for novelty but lack their [designs from George Nelson's era] former power to enlighten" (Abercrombie 2000: 233). Nelson, he relates, was a designer that was concerned with specific problems and solutions over his career but especially exhibited a "concern for design principles rather than for their visual expression" (Abercrombie 2000). The postwar interior's ability to enlighten comes directly from its emphasis on principles, its basis in theoretical discussions of its time, its shared intents, and its practitioners' diverse yet earnest efforts to use interior design as a medium to explore these ideas.

   This book hopefully raises interest in what one would find if they continued to look behind the physical manifestations and documentation of interior designs to reveal and understand the principles that contributed to their making. And if we investigated the designs being done today in that way, would we find a study of philosophy? An interest in the theories of vision? A deep-rooted connection to the tenets of the modern movement or a strong belief in its ability to impact humanity? I would guess that might not often be the case. I go further and suggest that perhaps we have lost that attachment to ideas that the field of interior design and modern design in general once had. One reason for this and that contemporary interior design may lack the "power to enlighten," as Stanley Abercrombie has noted, is the fact that while the interiors like those considered in this book, which serve as examples and inspiration for contemporary designs, have been documented visually and are numerously replicated in history texts, the ideas that shaped them remain largely unknown, having been left behind or overlooked. The Knoll Look, for example, is still easily recognizable and enjoys emulation if not almost iconic status, but the theoretical considerations that may have shaped it are not commonly discussed. Likewise, George Nelson's humanistic stance is not necessarily embedded in the numerous contemporary uses and installations of his platform bench. The stylistic devices and much-admired modernism of Richard Neutra, when replicated today, may totally be aesthetic and omit the preparatory research he did about and with his clients and his focus on their health and well-being. A new interior that emulates the layered visual qualities of the Eames House does not necessarily understand nor care about how its model reflected specific concerns about visual communication. And a new user of American Modern china or a Cowboy Modern chair probably does not understand the Wrights' zealous concern about being American. And so, while designs of the postwar period considered here are presently enjoying new and continued appreciation and emulation, their use and the new interpretations they inspire are most often stylistic and driven by aesthetics not idea. The lessons of these designers and the meanings of their designs have been disappeared as documentation of their "effects" rather than their "principles" continue to be brought forward into contemporary emulations of them, causing them, as Abercrombie has aptly pointed out, to fall short of their models.

   Why has this happened? The answer to this question may lie in considering the conditions that contributed to the transformation of design, particularly modern design and interior design, into a successful business enterprise in the mid-century period and after. The need to make a profit, to compete in markets, and to encourage buyers to buy design created a different impetus for designing than wanting to "create a more humane environment" as Nelson did or make a "visual culture that helps people better negotiate the world" like the Eameses. The use of modern design and interior design specifically was seen as an important strategy for continued economic growth in the postwar period and the development of products and places appropriate for a "new American way of life." Richard Nixon in his infamous "kitchen debate" with Khruschev in 1959 had argued that "American superiority in the cold war rested not on weapons but on the secure, abundant family life of the modern suburban home" (May 1988: 17). Historian Elaine Tyler May relates that in this modern home "adorned and worshipped by their inhabitants, women would achieve their glory and men would display their success. Consumerism was not an end in itself; it was the means for achieving individuality, leisure and upward mobility" (May 1988). May reports that in the five years after the Second World War consumer spending increased 60 percent with the amount spent on household furnishing and appliances cresting at 240 percent, while one million new housing units were produced each year (May 1988: 165). At the same time American businesses were prospering and expanding and sought updated facilities, buildings, offices, and furnishings that would portray their success. Modern was considered the most appropriate style for the new and renovated homes, businesses and new products and home furnishings that were created during this period. The rising consumerism of the postwar period that fed the wave of creativity exhibited in mid-century modern design and the desire for modern products happens at the same time, if not as the result of the efforts of the designers featured here.

When Edgar Kaufmann jr. inaugurated the Good Design shows of the 1950s, he further codified the link between modern design and consumerism. By ignoring the implied criticism of their commercialism and of being too "low-brow" because of that, the Good Design shows allowed Kaufmann to advocate for a "more populist" and "domesticated" modernism that successfully reached an audience of thousands more Americans than normally would have been involved in the more high-brow design shows that the Museum also promoted (Riley and Eigen 1994: 155). He constructed and executed the Good Design shows knowing from his experiences with his family's Pittsburgh department store that there was a market for this genre of products. Journals, media, and department stores also understood this and supported this urging of consumerism as well as the popularity of modern design.

As America transformed its war production into a consumer economy it created an unprecedented period of growth and prosperity. An important aspect of this growth was that its benefits extended quickly down and through the population creating more wealth per person and allowing many people to rise out of the lower working class to a substantial middle class with money to spend on goods and services. *Life* magazine declared in 1954, "Never before so much for so few" referring not to a privileged elite, but to the reality of lowest birthrate in the country's history (Hine 1986: 15). Designers like the Wrights in their *Guide to Easier Living*, Kaufmann and the

Museum of Modern Art, and popular magazines like *House Beautiful* set standards for consumption and models of good taste for the modern interior as America entered into what Thomas Hine calls the era of Populuxe, "One of history's great shopping sprees," (Hine: 3) which was, "the result of an unprecedented ability to acquire, reaching well down into the working class, to the sort of people who had historically been able to have only a few mean objects" (Hine: 12). But these consumers, in the frenzy of their new spending ability, appeared to care more about cost, accessibility, and quantity rather than quality. Hine says, "These people did not acquire the good simple objects many tastemakers advocated. They had had it with simple and they wanted more" (Hine: 13). As a result an expanded definition of "modern" grew out of this impetus, and the plethora of new smaller-scale housing with modern, more open interiors being built in America's new suburbs across the country such as Levittown on Long Island, Panorama City in Los Angeles, and Park Forest in Chicago needed to be furnished and decorated. The idea of having a "modern" home appealed to a population making a new start and separating themselves from the burden of indicators of historicism and their parents' kind of past, but the high design and ideals of the prominent designers considered here was soon found not to specifically be necessary. An ever-growing list of new furniture manufacturers rushed in to serve this market, often creating strange and less expensive, generic kinds of "knock-offs" of prominent modern designs and interiors, such as the furniture my mother was able to own. Competition became fierce and in this effort the market was expanded to give consumers a large variety of choices, in price, color, and features—essentially giving them whatever they thought they desired. Refrigerators, sinks, and toilets began to be made into a rainbow of color choices. Patterns and textiles assumed new color and decorativeness as needed. Modern furniture assumed traditional details like button tufting and brocaded fabric, and the language of modern design expanded to include words like "contemporary," "transitional," and "romanticism," which allowed eclectic mixes of styles from all periods to be considered as part of a modern interior. And so, while the modern designs of the Eameses, Knoll, and others included here were subtly pushed over time into the more ethereal realm of "high-brow" by the critical acclaim of experts and writers such as Russell Lynes in his later editions of his book *The Tastemakers*, the Museum of Modern Art in their continuing Good Design shows, the Walker Art Museum's Every Day Art Gallery, and *Arts and Architecture* magazine's Case Study House program, a new source of modern design referred to generically as "Grand Rapids" (named after America's foremost manufacturing center of mass-market modern furniture) promoted the creation of a more eclectic and less expensive modern designated as "low middle-brow," which became the genre that fed the majority of Americans desire for being modern.

The resulting boom in modern design being manufactured in this sector and the rampant consumerism and quick pace of demand and change that followed it had to inevitably tear apart the slower theoretical approaches of the designers considered here. In order to be successful in the maelstrom of marketing, production, and sales of designed products that grew out of the postwar period, designers had no choice but to deal with market forces, user desires, and trends rather than philosophies and theories. The fast pace and frenzy of these activities could not possibly support an extended and thoughtful design process. George Nelson referred to it as the development of a "Kleenex culture," which "rejects old things to get bored with new ones" and noted the problematic deficiency and damage done to thoughtful design development: "The concomitant emphasis on novelty as *the* desirable quality," he criticized, "tends to obscure the facts of design development and the understanding of superior performance in this area" (Nelson 1957: 12). As a result, modern design lost its impetus as a force for exploration and expression of a modern world and, in the hands of the new market forces, lost also its credibility as a force for social change. By 1956 a *House Beautiful* article was able to state categorically that modern "had played itself out" and "as it had come to be known in the last few decades, soon became incapable of anything but repetition of a few geometric forms. Designers have failed to find any inspiration in it as a point of departure." Because of that, it declared, a new era of "Romanticism" had begun. Modernism's over-speculation and over-production had drained the life out of it, making the way for the highly patterned, decorative, colorful, and eclectic interiors of the 1970s that would be shaped by design decisions made by manufacturers and consumers rather than designers. Unfortunately, the efforts of the designers highlighted here are not discarded in this new wave but appropriated for new uses. In a 1956 ad for Armstrong flooring, for example, a vivid red, blue, and white color scheme dominates a modern interior showing their flooring product and is adorned with a Nelson platform bench, in this instance painted a garish blue to match the scheme, something Nelson certainly would have deplored. At the same time, we can see a range of versions of molded plywood and fiberglass chairs and other furniture copying Eames, Nelson, Knoll, and Wright's contributions, while the liberal and sometimes purely decorative use of zebra and cow hides, folk art, and dried plants inspired by the Eames and Wrights enter the modern interior's vocabulary as standard devices. The tearing of these efforts out of their original context and away from the designers' intent to make them serve the needs of this new consumerism shifts our understanding of them far away from their principles to use only their effects in very undiscriminating ways. The blatant scavenging of these designers' work and the distancing if not total disregard for the design's embedded concepts and desire to shape modern life must have been discouraging. This may be why designers like Richard Neutra, who was committed to creating thoughtful interiors that were concerned with health, was no longer valued as he had been and even began to be ridiculed; or why Russel Wright retired to his estate in Manitoga to continue his experiments on his own home; or why George Nelson turned more to writing to expound his ideas than to design itself; or why the Eameses turned to film and media to continue their explorations and Florence Knoll retired.

The second key factor for this decline of emphasis on "principles" rather than "effects," in some ways also caused by consumerism, was the rise of photography as a way of knowing design. Photography during this period became a very powerful and largely used tool to not only document design but also promote its consumption. The inclusion of slick photographs of architecture, interiors, and products by skilled photographers such as Julius Shulman in accessible magazines such as *Better Homes and Gardens, Life* and *The Saturday Evening Post* made photographs of modern design also a consumable object, in addition to and sometimes as replacement of the designed objects themselves. The work of the designers considered here became iconic parts of design history because of the photographs taken of them were aesthetically beautiful, provocative, and generally more accessible than the real projects. In the case of interior design which is not replicable as a product for sale, and in many cases does not still exist or has become a display or museum setting that one might have to travel great distance to physically visit, the photograph documenting those designs acquires its own importance. Photographs of the Eames house and furniture, for example, become objects of desire, which can be consumed in their visual form as photography, and are even more accessible than the physical space and products, which one might never be able to encounter. In this way photography mediated products of modern design and removed them from their actual use—cropped, edited, contained, and in some ways tamed and modified them and our knowledge of them. The classic photographs of Julius Shulman of many of the Neutra and Eames projects, for example, are stunning works of art in themselves, but glamorize and distance the projects from their concerns that fed their making. One cannot feel the heat of the desert in Shulman's photograph of Neutra's Miller House, or know how the design works to integrate its user with that landscape, nor of the designer's real concern for the comfort and well-being of its occupants. Instead we can know only the flat beautiful image of the house in the very contrived framing of the photograph. This is good and bad of course. Good because it provides marvelous accessible documentation of houses, spaces, and products for history and for the general public to know, while their slickness and beauty only increases their desirability to consumers who might want to emulate or use those products. But bad at the same time, because the mediation that photography performs diminishes, if not disappears totally, the substance and the trace of the very deliberate thought processes that created that design. Edgar Kaufmann jr. admits in the introduction to his booklet, "What is Modern Interior Design," that the photograph of an interior was often the arbiter of a work being recognized as significant and included in his publication: "Some excellent and well-known modern interiors were omitted," he says, "because too many photographs were required to explain their worth, others, because no satisfactory photos were available" (Kaufmann jr. 1953: 3). In my own experience of constructing this book, I can discuss only examples from the photographs I could find and were available to me. For the number included here, I am sure there are an equal number or more of interiors unknown to me because there are no available photographs of them. Since photography has become a main way that we see, learn about, and consume design, it has at the same time limited our way of knowing it and has worked its toll on our ability to understand the making of those products and spaces and the ideas that shaped them.

The rise of intertextuality in the postmodern period and our new habits of relying on the internet to find inspiration in images by using Pinterest or Google also have laid waste the process of developing concepts and design in the way that the mid-century modern designers featured here might have done. In 1957 George Nelson defined the designer's responsibility as:

> To develop an artist's awareness of the modern world, and by this I mean total awareness which integrates the outlooks of the scientist, the mathematician and everyone else who is acting creatively ... it is our responsibility as artists in industry to make these things manifest, and thus to extend through our work a growing comprehension of the modern world. Until we learn to comprehend it, we haven't a chance of learning how to control it. (Nelson 1957: 7)

Nelson, as other designers of this period, believed that design had a serious role to play in navigating and understanding the modern world and that this required a committed involvement and expansive design process. He further stated, "A good design is one which achieves integrity—that is, unity or wholeness—in balanced relation to its environment. The reason good design is hard to come by is that its creation demands a high degree of emotional and intellectual maturity and such people are not found too often" (Nelson 1957: 11). But the mechanisms of being able to become this type of person and designer were largely stripped away by the forces described here. And so, rather than fully engaging in exploration and reading (as Nelson did), or physically collecting (as the Eames did), or studying nature and human behavior (like the Wrights and Neutra did), or traveling worldwide to have a variety of direct experiences (as Knoll did), contemporary designers in their fast-paced, market-driven environment often have to rely heavily on the mediated ideas they find in replications of things, mostly in photographs, rather than in real experience. This mid-century period of modern design in American, which produced some of the greatest, most respected, and still appreciated brand of modern interior design, may have been the last age of design thinkers who had the luxury and the inclination to immerse themselves in the world of ideas and to use design as a tool to explore those ideas. Unfortunately, the large expansive process of exploration they felt was needed to design and the slowness that it takes to discover, accumulate, and process in the way mid-century designers did is for the most part largely gone, available in some ways only to the design student or educator who has the time and inclination to explore a more extensive and thorough kind of concept development as an educational experience. The documentary film that records the dismantling of the Eames office "901: 45 Years of Working" created by the Eameses' grandson Eames Demetrios in 1989 in some ways documents this loss. In this film, the plethora of objects and collections in the office that were used in the Eameses' design process is displayed, disassembled, and removed. In that taking away one realizes both the depth of the research and the exploration of the couple as well as the significant role this accumulation of objects, texts, and documentations played in that process. Forty-five years of research and thinking are embodied in these. The sheer number of things is remarkable, and in many ways could certainly never be replaced or replicated. Today a design office might never stay in the same place or be in existence that long, and the main requirements for working might only be desks, chairs, computers, and the internet. Because of this I suspect that if one was to look for the concepts behind contemporary interior design, one would not be able to find the same rich pool of ideas that fed these mid-century modern designers. And so I propose that this period of mid-century modern was truly a golden age of design, particularly of interior design, perhaps never to be repeated. These designs endure, are valued, and have become "classics," not just because of their visual attributes but as a result of the richness of the designer's thought process and research that fed those visual attributes—their "principles" rather than their "effects." By bringing the ideas behind the work of the designers considered here to light, this book hopes to makes available a more accurate understanding of interior design and all design during this period. But more, it hopes to acknowledge if not privilege the method, commitment, seriousness, and depth of the practice that created this emergent phase of interior design and hopefully provide current design practice with both inspiration and models for how to use this practice to create more purposeful and important work in today's contemporary context.

Notes

Introduction

1   A note on the word "modern." As Lawrence E. Cahoone points out in his introduction to the edited volume *From Modernism to Postmodernism: An Anthology*, the word "modern" "has been used in various periods and places to distinguish contemporary from traditional ways" (p. 11), whereas "modernism" has been used in a "famously ambiguous way" to refer to the philosophy or culture of the modern period as a whole or to a historical period of the arts from about 1850 to 1950. When I use the word "modern" in this book I use it to describe both a society and a kind of design that wish to identify themselves as different from traditional and historical notions and that attempt to be both progressive and appropriate for its time period.

2   It must be noted that issues of gender are implicit in the discussion of interior decoration and interior design, but I wish to acknowledge that this inscription of gender on the concepts of interior decoration and design is not the primary focus of my discussion here and will not be elaborated on. For further discussion of gender and interior design see Lucinda Kaukas, "Decoration as Modernism's Other: Re-reading the Texts of Early Modern Design and Architecture," in *Cultural and Artistic Upheavals in Modern Europe: 1848 to 1945*, eds Sally Metzler and Elizabeth Lovett College, Cummer Studies, Volume I (Jacksonville, FL: Cummer Museum of Art, 1996), 149–63 and Lucinda Kaukas Havenhand "A View from the Margin: Interior Design," in *Design Issues* (Cambridge, MA: MIT Press, Volume XX, Number 4, Autumn 2004), 32–42.

3   For a more detailed discussion of the problems of interior design identity see Lucinda Kaukas Havenhand "A View from the Margin: Interior Design," in *Design Issues*. (Cambridge, MA: MIT Press, Volume XX, Number 4, Autumn 2004), 32–42.

Chapter 1

1   Russell Lynes, "Forward," in William Hennessey, *Russel Wright: American Designer* (New York: Gallery Association of New York, 1983). Numerous authors discuss the unusual spelling of Russel Wright's first name. In his foreword, Russell Lynes relates the story that a printing company inadvertently

misspelled Wright's name as 'Russel' on some letterhead that they had
printed for the designer. Russell Wright found the new spelling distinctive and
decided to change his name to Russel Wright to match his new stationery.

2   In chapter 1 of their book, the Wrights imply that "feelings of inferiority"
and even juvenile delinquency and frequency of divorce can be ameliorated
by the design of a home. See Russel and Mary Wright, *Guide to Easier
Living* (New York: Simon and Schuster, 1950; reprint Layton, UT: Gibbs Smith
Publisher, 2003), 1–10. Page numbers refer to reprint.

Chapter 2

1   The Sweets catalogs is a compilation of building products and specifications
used by architects and engineers to specify pre-manufactured building
components, fixtures, and materials. It is updated on a yearly basis.

2   Sylvia Lavin, *Form Follows Libido: Architecture and Richard Neutra
in a Psychoanalytical Culture* (Cambridge, MA: MIT Press, 2004), 3.
"Environmental design" is a term developed in the postwar period to label
a whole subset of activities that concerned itself with the scientific study of
how people acted and interacted within their environments and the design
of architecture, interiors, and furniture in response to these studies. Its
impetus came from the belief that such studies would enable designers to
better understand human needs and, through this understanding, be able
to design more life-enhancing space. The development of life-enhancing
and humane space was seen as a method of "healing" the ills of a society
fraught with modern anxieties and problems.

3   Sadly, Neutra and his wife Dione eventually came to the conclusion that they
could not provide that environment and his son was institutionalized in the
late 1940s.

4   Perhaps inspired by his father, Neutra's son Raymond became a medical
doctor specializing in environmental medicine.

5   Julius Shulman was young photographer struggling to establish his career
in the post-depression years when he met Richard Neutra. Shulman's
documentation of Neutra's house for Grace Miller in Palm Beach and
subsequent work for him and other designers and architects catapulted him
to the forefront of architectural photography. See Peter Gössel, ed., *Julius
Shulman: Architecture as Photography* (Cologne: Benedikt Taschen Verlag
GmbH, 1998).

Chapter 3

1   For many years, only Charles Eames was given credit for this work even
though the couple always acknowledged their shared input. As Ray

Eames reported in an interview with Pat Kirkham in 1983, "it was a full collaboration. One can't say Charles did this bit. Ray did this bit." (Pat Kirkham, "Introducing Ray Eames," *Furniture History,* v.26 (1990), 135). Recent work by their grandson, Eames Demetrios, and others has further established a clear pattern of collaboration between the Eameses in each project undertaken. Charles's role often involved being the lead designer and meeting with clients and the public, while Ray's seemed to center more on keeping the office and projects running smoothly.

2   The Eameses kept a file with the Kepes correspondence that includes notes and letters between Ray and Charles Eames and György and Juliet Kepes. The Kepes refer to Charles intimately as "Charlie" and sign their correspondence with "love" and make frequent reference to their meetings and affection for each other. Eames Archive, Library of Congress, Box 61, Folder 6.

3   Ray Eames attended Hofmann's school and was lifelong friends with Mercedes Carles who married Herbert Matter.

Chapter 4

1   Although an advocate of "loving," Fromm was also equally concerned about understanding the nature of aggression and the destructive tendencies of mankind. This was perhaps inspired by the behavior of the Nazis, whose rise to power forced him to emigrate from Germany. The culmination of Fromm's study of this was his 1973 publication *The Anatomy of Human Destructiveness.* Fromm was also an ardent peace activist until his death. Nelson as a lifelong friend surely knew of these activities and concerns.

2   Perhaps inspired by or resonating with the philosophy of Erich Fromm. Fromm's biographer Rainer Funk relates that the Fromm advocated strongly that "those who preach progressive ideas must practice them," a viewpoint that was instilled in him by his early study with Rabbi Nehemiah Aton Nobel. Rainer Funk, *Erich Fromm: His Life and Ideas* (New York: Continuum International Publishing Group, Inc., 2000), 38.

3   Koans are seemingly meaningless and often bizarre dialogs or questions used in Zen practice whose answers involve a transformation of perspective or consciousness, which are practiced for the purpose of expanding the mind and one's understanding of reality.

Chapter 5

1   For the sake of clarity, Florence Knoll born Florence Schust and later to become Florence Knoll Bassett will be called Florence Knoll for the entirety of this chapter.

2   The term "Knoll Look" was first applied to Knoll's design by *Interiors* magazine in 1951 (see "Knoll Associates Move into the Big Time," *Interiors* 110 (May 1951), 74–83, 152). Rather than being a pejorative term, the word "look" was applied by the design magazines to identify specific design trends. A 1949 issue of *Interiors*, for example, uses the terms "handicraft look," "machine look," and "biomorphic look," to distinguish the three major design influences of note during this period. See "Modern Furniture, Its Nature, Its Sources, and Its Probable Future," *Interiors* 108 (July 1949), 76–117.

Suggested Readings

Abercrombie, S. (2000), *George Nelson: The Design of Modern Design*, Cambridge, MA: MIT Press.

Albrecht, D., Schonfeld, R., and Shapiro, L.S. (2001), *Russel Wright: Creating American Lifestyle*, New York: Harry N. Abrams.

Blaser, W. (1977), *Mies van der Rohe: Principles and School*, Basel: Birkhäuser Verlag.

Blaser, W. (1994), *Mies van der Rohe: The Art of Structure*, New York: Whitney Library of Design.

Carpenter, E.K. (1979), "A Tribute to Charles Eames," 25th Annual Design Review, *Industrial Design*, New York: Whitney Library of Design.

Christ-Janer, A. (1948), *Eliel Saarinen*, Chicago, IL: University of Chicago Press.

Conant Ball Sales Tips (n.d.), Box 5, Russel Wright Papers, Syracuse University Library Special Collections, Syracuse, New York.

Conrads, U., ed. (1986), *Programs and Manifestoes on 20th-Century Architecture*, Cambridge, MA: MIT Press.

Danto, A. (2000), "Riegl Bearing," *Art Forum International* 39, no. 1 September.

Davenport, Charles (1962), "Designer Charles Eames: Chairs, Fairs and Films," *Los Angeles Magazine* 3: 24–7.

Demetrios, E. (2002), *An Eames Primer*, London: Thames and Hudson.

Drexler, A. and Hines, T. (1982), *The Architecture of Richard Neutra: From International Style to California Modern*, New York: Museum of Modern Art.

Eames, C. (1950), "Life in a Chinese Kite," *Architectural Forum* September: 94.

Eames, C. (1957), "The Experimental House, by Nelson and Chadwick," *Architectural Record* 122 December: 136–42.

Eames, C. (1974), "Language of Vision: The Nuts and Bolts," *Bulletin of the America Academy of Arts and Sciences* October: 18–19.

Eames, C. (1977) Notes for Frank Nelson Doubleday Lecture at Smithsonian Eames Archive, Box 217, Folder 14, 5.

Fehrman, C. and Fehrman, K. (1987), *Postwar Interior Design: 1945–1960*, New York: Van Nostrand Reinhold.

Franck, F. (1978), *Zen and Zen Classics*, New York: Vintage Books.

Fromm, Eric (1955), *The Sane Society*, New York: Rinehart & Company.

Funk, R. (2000), *Erich Fromm: His Life and Ideas*, New York: Continuum International Publishing Group, Inc.

Gill, F. (1940) *Autobiography*, Cape May, NJ: Cape Publishing.

Girard, A. and Laurie, W.D. eds (1949), *An Exhibition for Modern Living*, Detroit, MI: Detroit Institute of Arts.

Goldstein, B. and McCoy, E. (1990), *Arts and Architecture: The Entenza Years*, Cambridge, MA: MIT Press.

Golec, M. (2002), "A Natural History of a Disembodied Eye: The Structure of György Kepes's Language of Vision," *Design Issues* 18, no. 2, Spring: 3–16.

Gössel, P., Leuthäuser, G., and Sembach, K. (1991), *Twentieth-Century Furniture Design*, Cologne: Benedikt Taschen Verlag.

Havenhand, L.K. (2004), "A View from the Margin: Interior Design," in *Design Issues*, Cambridge, MA: MIT Press, XX, No. 4, Autumn: 32–42.

Havenhand, L.K. (2006) "American Abstract Art and the Interior Design of Ray and Charles Eames," *Journal of Interior Design* 31, no. 2: 29–42.

Havenhand, L.K. (2014) "Russel and Mary Wright's *Guide to Easier Living* and the 'New American Way of Life,'" *Interiors* 5, no. 2: 199–218.

Hennessey, W. (1983), *Russel Wright: American Designer*, New York: Gallery Association of New York.

Hine, T. (1986), *Popluxe*, New York: Alfred A. Knopf.

Hines, T. (1982), *Richard Neutra and the Search for Modern Architecture: A Biography and History*. New York: Oxford University Press.

Hobbs, R. (1993), *Lee Krasner*, New York: Abbeville Press.

Hunter, S. (1982), "Introduction," in *Hans Hofmann*, New York: Abrams.

Innes, C. (2005), *Designing Modern America: Broadway to Main Street*, New Haven, CT: Yale University Press.

Isenstadt, S. (2000), "Neutra and Architectural Consumptions," in Goldhagen, S. and Legault, R. eds *Anxious Modernisms*, Cambridge, MA: MIT Press, 103.

Izutsu, A. (1992), *The Bauhaus: A Japanese Perspective and a Profile of Hans and Florence Schust Knoll*, trans. Brian Harrison. Tokyo: Kajima Institute.

Kammen, M. (1991), *Mystic Chords of Memory: The Transformation of Tradition in American Culture*, New York: Alfred A. Knopf.

Kaufmann, jr. E. (1949) in Alexander Girard and W.D. Laurie, ed., *An Exhibition for Modern Living*, Detroit Institute of Arts.

Kaufmann, jr. E. (1953), *What Is Modern Interior Design?* New York: Museum of Modern Art.

Kepes, G. (1944), *Language of Vision*, Chicago, IL: Paul Theobald and Co.

Kepes, G. (1948), "Form and Motion," *Arts and Architecture*, July/August.

Kepes, G. (1965), *Education of Vision*, New York: Braziller.

Kepes, G., ed. (1966), *Sign, Image, Symbol*, New York: Braziller.

Kirkham, P. (1995), *Charles and Ray Eames: Designers of the Twentieth Century*, Cambridge, MA: MIT Press.

Knight, P. (1967), *The Radiant City*, New York: Orion Press.

Knoll Associates, Inc., (1961), "Knoll International, Ltd," Oversize brochure.

Koren, L. (1994), *Wabi-Sabi for Artists, Designers, Philosophers and Poets*, Berkeley, CA: Stone Bridge Press.

Lambert, P., ed. (2001), *Mies in America*, New York: H.N. Abrams.

Lange, A. (2006), "This Year's Model: Representing Modernism to the Post-war American Corporation," *Journal of Design History* 19, no. 3.

Lavin, S. (2004), *Form Follows Libido: Architecture and Richard Neutra in a Psychoanalytical Culture*, Cambridge, MA: MIT Press.

Leet, S. (2004), *Richard Neutra's Miller House*, New York: Princeton Architectural Press.

Makovsky, P. (2001), "Shu U," *Metropolis* 20, no. 11: 122.

Makovsky, P. (2004), "The Eames Experience," *Metropolis*, December.

144 SUGGESTED READINGS

Marguardt, V. (1970), "Gyorgy Kepes: New Criteria of Art in a Scientific-Industrial Environment," MA Thesis, University of Wisconsin, Madison.

Marlin, William, ed. (1989) *Nature Near: Late Essays of Richard Neutra*, Santa Barbara, CA: Capra Press.

May, Elaine Tyler. (1988) *Homeward Bound: American Families in the Cold War Era*, New York: Basic Books, Inc.

McCoy, E. (1973), "An Affection for Objects," *Progressive Architecture*, August: 67.

McCoy, E. (1977), *Case Study Houses: 1945–1962*, Los Angeles: Hennessey & Ingalls, Inc.

Mckellar, S. and Sparke, P., eds (2004), *Interior Design and Identity*, Manchester, UK: Manchester University Press.

Miller, R.C. (1983), "Interior Design and Furniture," in *Design in America: The Cranbrook Vision 1925–1950*, New York: Harry Abrams.

Moffett, K. (1973), *Meier-Graefe as Art Critic*, Munich: Prestel-Verlag.

Mumford, L. (1930), "American Condescension and European Superiority," *Scribner's Magazine*, 87: 525.

Nelson, G. (1936), "Architects of Europe Today: Eugene Beaudouin, France," *Pencil Points*, March: 133.

Nelson, G. and Wright, Henry. (1945), *Tomorrow's House: How to Plan Your Postwar Home*, New York: Simon and Shuster.

Nelson, G. (1946), "Wright's Houses," *Fortune* 34: 116–25.

Nelson, G. (1948), "Problems of Design: The Dead-End Room," *Interiors* 108: 84–7.

Nelson, G. (1954), "The Georgia Experiment: An Industrial Approach to Problems of Education," lecture dated October 1954, marked as "unread" quoted in Abercrombie, 149.

Nelson, G. (1957), *Problems of Design*, New York: Whitney Publications.

Nelson, G. (1960), "Impressions of Japan," *Holiday*, February: 67.

Nelson, G. (1973) "The End of Architecture," *Architecture Plus*, April, 551.

Nelson, G. (1979), "Peak Experiences and the Creative Act," in *George Nelson On Design*, New York: Whitney Library of Design, 15–16.

Nelson, G. (1984), "Reflections on *Home-Psych*", *Interior Design*, March.

Neuhart, J. and Neuhart, M. (1994), *Eames House*, Berlin: Ernst and Sohn.

Neumeyer, F. (1991), *The Artless World: Mies van der Rohe on the Building Art*, Cambridge, MA: MIT Press.

Neutra, D. (1986), *Richard Neutra Promise and Fulfillment 1919–1932: Selections from the Letters and Diaries of Richard and Dione Neutra*, Carbondale, IL: Southern Illinois University Press.

Neutra, R. (1954), *Survival by Design*, New York: Oxford University Press.

Neutra, R. (1962), *Life and Shape*, New York: Appleton Century Crofts.

Okakura, K. (1989), *The Book of Tea*, New York: Kodansha International.

Ortega y. Gasset, J. (1941), *History as a System and Other Essays Toward a Philosophy of History*, New York: Norton.

Ortega y. Gasset, J. (2004) Obras, completes, Vol. 1, Madrid: Taurus Fundacion.

Pulos, A. (1988), *The American Design Adventure. 1940–1975*, Cambridge, MA: The MIT Press.

Riley, T. and Eigen, E. (1994), "Between the Museum and the Marketplace: Selling Good Design," in *The Museum of Modern Art at Mid-Century: At Home and Abroad*, New York: Museum of Modern Art.

Saarinen, Eero (1956), "The Maturing Modern" *Time,* 2 July, 57.

Saarinen, E. (1929), "Modern Features of Art," *Pencil Points* 10: 202.

Saarinen, E. (1948), A *Search for Form: A Fundamental Approach to Art*, New York: Reinhold Publishing Corp.

Scheerbert, P. (1964), *Glassarchitektur* in Ulrich Conrads, ed., *Programs and Manifestos on Twentieth Century Architecture*, Cambridge, MA: MIT Press.

Schilpp, P., ed. (1951), *The Philosophy of Alfred North Whitehead*, New York: Tudor Publishing Company 2nd edition.

Schlesinger Jr., A. (1949), *The Vital Center*, Boston, MA: Houghton-Mifflin.

Suckow, Ruth (1930), "The Folk in American Life," *Scribner's Magazine*, 88.

Suzuki, D. (1989), *Zen and Japanese Culture*, Princeton, NJ: Princeton University Press.

Tate, A. and Smith, C.R. (1986), *Interior Design in the 20th Century*, New York: Harper and Row.

Tigerman, B. (2005), "'I Am not a Decorator': Florence Knoll, The Knoll Planning Unit, and the Making of the Modern Office," MA Thesis, University of Delaware.

Warren, V.L. (1964), "Woman Who Led an Office Revolutions Rules an Empire of Modern Design," *New York Times*, September 1: 40.

Whitehead, A.N. (1932), "Immortality," in *Science and the Modern World*, Cambridge: Cambridge University Press.

Whitehead, A.N. (1957), *Aims of Education*, New York: The Free Press. Originally printed in 1929.

Wigley, M. (1995), *White Walls, Designer Dresses: The Fashioning of Modern Architecture*, Cambridge, MA: MIT Press.

Wright, R. (2001), *Russel Wright: Good Design Is for Everyone: In His Own Words*, Manitoga, NY: The Russel Wright Design Center; Rizzoli International Publications.

Wright, R. and Wright, M. (1950), *Guide to Easier Living*, New York: Simon and Schuster.

Wright, R. (1941), *American Way Sales Manual.*

Index

Note: Locators with letter "n" refer to notes.